Learning to Lead

Learning to Lead

A Workbook
On Becoming A Leader

UPDATED EDITION

Warren Bennis

Joan Goldsmith

PERSEUS BOOKS

Reading, Massachusetts

Library of Congress Cataloging-in-Publication Data

Bennis, Warren G.
    Learning to lead : a workbook on becoming a leader / Warren
Bennis, Joan Goldsmith. — Rev. ed.
      p.   cm.
    Includes bibliographical references and index.
    ISBN 0-201-31140-2 (alk. paper)
    1. Leadership. 2. Management. I. Goldsmith, Joan. II. Title.
HD57.7.B463   1997
658.4'092—dc21   97-17568
                                                    CIP

Perseus Books is a member of the Perseus Books Group

Cover design by Suzanne Heiser
Set in 11/13 Garamond #3 by Maple-Vail Book Manufacturing Group

3 4 5 6 7 8 9   0201009998

Perseus Books are available at special discounts for bulk purchases in the U.S. by corporations, institutions, and other organizations. For more information, please contact the Corporate, Government, and Special Sales Department at Addison Wesley Longman, One Jacob Way, Reading, MA 01867, or call (800) 238-9682.

Find us on the World Wide Web at
http://www.aw.com/gb/

For our children who are the leaders of our future.

Kate, John, Will, Nina, Eden, and Peter from Warren.

Nick, Elka, Sam, Shetu, and Tinku, Kristen and Glen,
Scott, Danny, Greg, Jacob, Adam, Emily, Chloe, Sarah,
Alexandra, and David from Joan.

Table of Contents

Preface xi

Acknowledgments xxi

Chapter 1—Leadership for a Successful Future 1

The Future Is in Their Hands 1

The Integrity of Leadership 3

Leaders, Not Managers. 4

Trust, Plus Vision, Plus Meaning 5

The Buried Treasure 6

An Empowered Work Force. 6

Leadership Can Be Learned 7

The Learning Plan of This Workbook. 9

The Distinctions between Manager and Leader—An Exercise 9

Your Leadership Assessment—An Exercise 14

Leadership Assessment Inventory—An Exercise 15

Your Leadership Agenda—An Exercise. 18

Chapter 2—How to Use This Workbook 21

The Reinvention of Self 21

Leadership of Your Own Life 23

The Inner Voice 24

Self-Reflection 26

Personal Values for Effective Leaders—An Exercise 26

Personal Goals for Leaders—An Exercise 33

Group Leadership—An Exercise 35

Qualities That Support Group Leadership Development—An Exercise 37

Table of Contents

Chapter 3—The Leadership Crisis 41

The Loss of Leaders 41

The Leadership Crisis 44

Leaders from the Past—An Exercise 45

Leadership Myths—An Exercise 51

The Leadership Gap?—An Exercise 56

Leaders in Our Families—An Exercise 60

Leaders in Our Organization—An Exercise 64

Chapter 4—Knowing Yourself 69

The Beginning 69

The Shift in the Leadership Paradigm 71

Leaders Are Made by Learning How to Learn—An Exercise 73

Learning Modes—An Exercise 78

A Learning Style Presentation—An Exercise 80

Failure—The Springboard of Hope 82

Patterns of Failure—An Exercise 84

Leadership Checklist—An Exercise 92

The Lifeline—An Exercise 95

Chapter 5—Creating and Communicating a Vision 99

A Passionate Commitment to Vision 99

Alignment of Others to Your Vision 102

Your Organizational Vision—An Exercise 105

You in Your Vision—An Exercise 111

Communication and Your Vision—An Exercise 116

Chapter 6—Maintaining Trust through Integrity 119

Trust and Organizational Effectiveness 119

Qualities of Leadership—An Exercise 121

Support through Empathy 123

The Practice of Empathy—An Exercise 125

Trust through Consistent Integrity 132
Your Ethical Ten Commandments—An Exercise 135
The Integrity Gap—An Exercise....................................... 139

Chapter 7—Realizing Intention through Action 143
A Self-Assessment Prior to Action 144
Your Goals Statement—An Exercise 146
Commitment and Desire as Requisites for Action...................... 148
Commitments and Desires—An Exercise 150
Strategic Thinking.. 153
The Strategy Map—An Exercise 155
Power to Achieve Your Goals—Exercises............................... 161
Empowerment: A Conclusion.. 165

Books on Leadership: An Annotated Bibliography...................................... 167

References.. 177

Index.. 181

Preface

In which we establish the critical need for leadership at all levels of society, invite the reader's partnership in building leaders, and preview the structure of this book as a learning tool.

Ultimately, man should not ask what the meaning of his life is, but rather must recognize that it is he who is asked. In a word, each man is questioned by life, and he can only answer to life by answering for his own life, to life he can only respond by being responsible.

Viktor Frankl, *Man's Search for Meaning*

Writing and studying leadership has become a growth industry in recent years, yet our cities seem to have sunk deeper into crisis, our communities are in turmoil, our political leaders of both parties are repeatedly charged with ethical violations, and the world's multiple crises demand the immediate attention they are not receiving.

It is plainly not enough to appeal to existing leaders, we need a higher quality of leadership among *all* our citizens. Each of us needs to take to heart Viktor Frankl's admonition that each of us must be responsible for our own lives, and for the life of our community and our world. We are questioned daily by life, which asks us whether we are willing and able to fulfill our potential and respond to the enormous demands we face as a society.

We have written this book in the belief that honest, capable, ethical leadership is possible for all of us, and to support you in your journey to more effective leadership. The process need not be arduous. E. B. White put the challenge in these terms. He once wrote, "I wake up every morning determined both to change the world and have one hell of a good time. Sometimes this makes planning the day a little difficult." Every leader today needs to respond to a similar wake-up call, to change the world and also have a good time doing it. Yes, it also makes planning more difficult.

If we do not see any need to change the world or improve the quality of our lives, we will not be motivated to become leaders. If we do not make the process enjoyable, we will not improve the quality of our lives. For this reason, the observations, anecdotes, and exercises of this workbook are written to focus on both large and small problems, and at the same time enable you to enjoy transforming yourself into a more effective leader.

Character and the Leadership Crisis

As you pursue the goal of transformation, we point out that the mission or goals of the leader cannot be separated from the means that are used to achieve them. In leadership, character counts. Our convictions about character-based leadership come from years of studies, teaching, observations, and interviews with leaders, and with the people near them—their direct reports and board members. We maintain that leadership *is* character. It is not just a superficial question of style, but has to do with who we are as human beings, and with the forces that have shaped us.

We also believe that character continually evolves as we continue to acquire, grow, and develop. In our work with organizations caught in the turmoil of change, we watch staff, managers, and executives demonstrate character-based leadership, and see them win and lose based not only on their knowledge of business conditions, but also on their knowledge of themselves. Ellen Dempsey, President of IMPACT II, the National Teacher's Network, describes the role character plays in teacher leadership:

> Heroism cannot exist as a singular force within a school; the solo hero will
> quickly be beaten back by the forces of mediocrity and status quo operating
> within the environment. The independent visionary hero must extend her
> or his individual vision to the team as a whole in order to truly establish
> and maintain systemic reform.

As we look at ways of improving ourselves as character-based leaders, we find that the process of becoming a leader is much the same as the process of becoming an integrated human being. For this reason, the process we champion in this book in leading you toward more effective leadership is highly personal. It offers you opportunities to examine your own life—past, present, and future—and suggests questions to answer, steps to take, and new ways to express yourself as an integrated adult.

The signs of a leadership crisis are alarming and persuasive. Witness the changes in leadership and direction in many of our most respected corporations. In politics, it is the same. The mood of the populace has deteriorated and become more angry, cynical, sometimes foul, and in a few horrifying cases even murderous. Those who ostensibly lead us only agree that things are getting worse, without providing us with convincing programs to make them better. We don't recall such a widespread loss of faith in our major institutions, even during the tumultuous 1960's.

One of the most obvious challenges facing leaders today is the incredible change taking place in technology and in globalization. These changes affect all corporations today and are creating great confusion. One CEO told us, "If you're not confused, you don't know what's going on." We are also having a harder time implementing change—partly due to the immense size of our corporations and government agencies, which limit our creativity and bureaucratize our imagination.

Joblessness is eating the core of our cities and creating a powerful demand for innovative and courageous leadership to provide employment and revitalization for our communities. Harvard Professor William Julius Wilson describes this challenge eloquently in his groundbreaking study of the urban crisis, *When Work Disappears:*

> Most workers in the inner city are ready, willing, able and anxious to hold a steady job. . . . We need long-term solutions that reduce the likelihood that a new generation of jobless workers would be produced from the youngsters now in school and preschool. We must break the cycle of joblessness and improve the youngsters' preparation for the new labor market in the global economy.

The issue of failed leadership extends beyond our cities. Around the globe, humanity faces three extraordinarily potent threats: the threat of annihilation as a result of nuclear accident or war, the threat of worldwide plague, and the threat of ecological catastrophe. These dangers raise a fourth threat: the failure of leadership to address these concerns. Although plague, nuclear holocaust, and ecological catastrophe are serious problems, the failure of leadership is in many ways more urgent and more dangerous because none of the other problems we face can be solved without it, and because it is insufficiently recognized and little understood.

Preface

With these crises in mind, and with "Where Have All the Leaders Gone?" playing in our heads, we have shaped this book. We do not offer magic formulas or quick cures, but we do provide a clear and effective framework for thinking about and developing our leadership talents that will help us take the necessary steps to resolve the leadership crisis that faces us.

In our view, we are each capable of creating ourselves as effective leaders. The challenge we pose to you, our partners in this venture, is to confront your doubts and hopes and to be willing to become a leader in your own life, so you can expand your capacity to make a contribution to the issues and crises we all face. The learning process is one that includes the pain of self-critical examination and the exhilaration of taking risks and reaching goals. As you commit to the learning process we have outlined in this workbook, we encourage you to explore your triumphs and disappointments as you emerge as a leader.

To begin to grapple with your own growth as a leader we ask you to begin with character and with a set of core competencies. By inviting you to consider what we have written in these pages and to participate in the exercises we propose, we are inviting you to look at *all* aspects of your life. The skills you develop through this process will not only enable you to become the leader you envision yourself being, but will also allow you to mature and expand your capacity to live life more fully and completely.

We believe that the true power of this book lies in your own self-discovery. We ask you to observe yourself closely, to activate your ability to learn, to reflect on your experiences, and to change life patterns that do not serve you in becoming the leader you want to be. In the book, we ask you to reflect openly on your life, and to assess yourself and your experiences honestly. We ask you to let down your guard, take a risk, and confront your life choices.

Four Personal Responsibilities

This is a book about leadership, but not leadership with a capital *L*. The problems we face are too complex, multilayered, numerous, and widespread for a small group of "Leaders" to have an impact. Our vision of leadership is one in which every person who reads this book, who applies the ideas, and who explores the activities can become a leader in his or her own life.

The problems of our cities require leaders on every block, in every church, in every community. The crisis in education calls for every parent, teacher, classroom aide, student, and administrator to create visions for their future, to inspire commitment, to foster creativity, and to stimulate achievement. The failures of our corporations demand leadership qualities from every staff member, every secretary, every salesperson, every accounts payable clerk, and every CEO, so as to catalyze enthusiasm, encourage risk taking, and create break-throughs in innovation. The future will work only when each of us *makes* it work.

Most of the organizations with which we work are undergoing substantial, even continuous change. Merger mania, reengineering righteousness, and downsizing depression grab hold of and twist everyone who gets caught in their grip. Our observations have taught us that no single leader can save the day. Truly successful leadership today requires teams, collabo-ration, diversity, innovation, and cooperation. Leadership has begun to take on a new di-mension. The leadership we are seeking is one that is empowering, supportive, visionary, problem-solving, creative, and shared. We are calling for a *continuum* of leadership that includes indirect leadership exerted through support and networking or scholarly studies or symbolic communication; and that extends to direct leadership of the sort that is exercised by world leaders through speeches and similar means. On that continuum, each of us can find a place and a means of expressing ourselves.

What do people want from their leaders? We have identified four demands that stand out from the rest, and have a deep relevance for tomorrow's organizations. What most constit-uents want from their leaders are:

1. Purpose, Direction, and Meaning

We cannot exaggerate the significance of a strong determination to achieve a goal, together with the conviction, passion, and unique point of view that establish the energy and direc-tion of the leader. Corporate leader Max DePree said, "The first task of a leader is to help define reality." That's another way of talking about purpose. Without a sense of alignment behind that purpose, we drift aimlessly. It cannot be any old purpose either, but must be one that galvanizes, energizes, and enthralls people. It has to have meaning and resonance. It also has to belong to *everyone* in the organization. The leader not only must have direction, but also must communicate it in such a way that ownership is created on every level and in every corner of the operation.

2. Trust

Leaders must generate and sustain trust. The trust factor is the social glue that binds commitment and promotes action necessary to produce results. Without it, you can't win. To trust other people, to have confidence in them, we need to see evidence of their compe-tence. Another aspect of trust is openness. We cannot overemphasize the importance of

Preface

encouraging openness, even dissent. Warren once received a letter from an executive who wrote: "We've got thousands of folks, union workers, who want the world to be the way it used to be, and they are very unwilling to accept any alternative forecast of the future." But the real problem was that there was no trust between the managers and the employees in that organization, and the executive was part of the problem. He was old-fashioned and command-and-control oriented, and could not generate trust among key stakeholders by including them in making decisions about the future.

3. Optimism

All leaders need to be purveyors of hope. Their optimism fascinates others because it is so pervasive and so powerful. It cannot be built on grand delusions or on phony grounds. Most of the leaders we have observed do not get stuck on their mistakes, problems, wrong turns, or mishaps. They see their errors as opportunities to learn and change, and as a growth process. Their optimism stems from their clear vision of the future and their commitment to get there and bring everyone on their team along for the ride.

4. Action and Results

The last quality common to leaders is a bias toward action. That is, leaders have the capacity to convert purpose and vision into action. It isn't enough just to have a great vision you can use to inspire people. It has to become manifest and real in some external way, and produce results. Most leaders are *pragmatic* dreamers and *practical* idealists. They step up and take their shots every day, perhaps knowing that, as hockey player Wayne Gretzky once said, "You miss 100 percent of the shots you *don't* take."

We have been fascinated by the problems facing leaders, and by the individuals who take them on, for most of our lives. We each began our study of leadership in our families, watching and learning all we needed to know to survive in a world of great upheaval and dramatic change. We have continued our deep involvement with leadership over the succeeding years. This workbook reflects our belief that all of us can continue to learn about leadership throughout our lives if we remain engaged in the exploration process. We encourage you to join a partnership that we propose in this workbook, so that we can make our experiences useful to you.

Many of you who are reading this book are engaged in this exploration of leadership, but are not yet serving in leadership positions. You may be students, community volunteers, or beginning the corporate climb at the bottom rung of the ladder. We hope you will find this book a welcome companion at the beginning of your journey. You may be a member of a high-performance team and find that leadership is a shared role among your team members and colleagues.

Our image of a solitary leader who is isolated at the top of the organization is out of date and no longer effective in dealing with the complex, often staggering problems we face worldwide. Most situations require leadership that is shared and inclusive, so that the greatest unity, which combines the best talents that are the most committed to discovering or inventing the best solutions, becomes the most successful. We invite you to expand your skills in sharing your leadership with others, and in providing access to leadership roles for your team mates.

We have given a great deal of thought to the need for leaders who can create solutions to the problems that seem to overwhelm our cities, our environment, our educational system, our corporations, and our families. Many of us can discuss the qualities of leaders, we can describe individuals who possess these talents, and we can recognize leadership when we see it. But few of us can sustain what we know through action. Few of us can be conscious of our true purpose and live it out day by day. Few of us can deploy our energies to enact the principles with which most of us would agree.

Our purpose in writing this workbook is to create a means by which each of us can translate our ideals and intentions into reality so that we can act on them in a way that makes a difference. As the novelist Nadine Gordimer observed in *The Burgher's Daughter,* "The real definition of loneliness is to live without social responsibility." It is our intention that your efforts to face the challenges of becoming a leader will lead to increased social responsibility and diminished loneliness and isolation.

Three Organizational Requirements

This new breed of leader faces the challenge of creating organizations, institutions, structures, and systems in which each person can apply his or her full human potential to discover solutions to seemingly overwhelming social problems. We lack effective, creative, and productive workplaces where, rather than suppressing ourselves, we are able to use our talents to express our contributions. What are the characteristics of these new organizations? We have identified three areas that convey both the potential and the difficulty of bringing these organizations out of crisis. The elements of the future organizations we envision are alignment with a common vision; empowerment of all involved; and a learning, inquiry-based, and reflective culture. This workbook will prepare you with the tools you will need to lead an organization with these characteristics from any place within it. As leaders, we need to understand these organizational elements better so that we can create and foster them where we work and live.

1. Alignment

Alignment with a common vision means having a sense of shared objectives and goals to which people can be dedicated. It has much to do with spirit and team atmosphere. It is "the vision thing." It is impossible to imagine the accomplishment of building AT&T, Ford, or Apple in the absence of a shared vision. Theodore Vail had a vision of universal telephone service that would take fifty years to bring about. Henry Ford envisioned common people, not just the wealthy, owning their own automobiles. Steven Jobs, Steve Wozniak, and their Apple co-founders saw the abilities of the computer to empower all people. A shared vision uplifts people's aspirations. Work becomes part of pursuing a larger purpose embodied in the organizations' products or services.

2. Empowerment

What we mean by empowerment of all involved really has to do with people sensing that they are at the center of things, rather than at the periphery; that everyone feels they make a difference to the success of the organization. Joan Dunlop, President of the International Women's Health Coalition, described the success of this empowerment when she cited the experience she and thousands of women from all over the world had who attended the United Nations Conference on Women in Beijing in 1995, as one in which "The power of women when allied was very effective in shifting the focus of most nations of the world from national security to human security."

Empowered individuals feel that what they do has meaning and significance. They have discretion and obligations and live in a culture of respect where they can actually do things without having to check through five levels of the hierarchy. Empowered organizations generate and sustain trust, flatten their structures, develop system-wide communication, and do a lot of it.

3. Learning culture

A learning, inquiry-based, and reflective culture is one where ideas and information come through unhampered by people who are worried or fearful. It means, first, being open to problem *finding*, not just problem solving. Adaptive, learning organizations can identify and find problems that are bothersome before they become crises. They understand that the simplicity that lies beyond complexity is the right kind of simplicity, and they beware the simplicity that comes before complexity. Second, they have or encourage discovery of the ideas and information needed to solve the problems. Third, they are not afraid to test these ideas. Fourth, a learning/inquiring organization provides opportunities to reflect on and evaluate past actions and decisions.

These three elements—alignment, empowerment, and a learning/inquiring culture—characterize most successful organizations. To implement these elements, we need a quality of leadership that differs from the commonly perceived model we have brought from the past. Post-bureaucratic organizations require leadership that is more interactional, more prone to surfacing healthy conflict and dissent, less averse to risk taking, more prone to embracing and learning from error, and much more encouraging of cross-functional teams. They require good coaches—leaders who are susceptible to listening to the ideas of colleagues, and who are able to abandon their egos to support the talents of others. New organizations are being decentralized into autonomous units. The decision-making power is being pushed down, and middle management is becoming less important. A flattened organization sets up autonomous teams that deliver the work without being over-managed. Management's role is to create a vision of the whole, and to empower others to reach it. This new organization requires self-discipline and emphasizes individual responsibility, relationships, and communication. Each person is responsible for communicating responsibly, which is a true quality of leadership.

We have designed the course of study in this book to enable you to become such a leader. We have written it as if we were working with you directly, as your consultant and coach. We have shared with you the interviews and stories about leaders we have gleaned from our research and experience. We have paced the activities for learning from our teaching and consulting experiences, so that they build on one another. We have also allowed room for your improvisation.

The workbook is organized in two parts. In the first part we make explicit our model of leadership and differentiate leadership from management; we establish the need for leaders in today's society; and we explain how you, the reader, can apply the activities and exercises of the book to your own life. In the second part we teach the competencies of leadership through building skills in self-reflection and continuous learning, envisioning the future, empowering others through communication, developing constancy by demonstrating ethical behavior, and deploying yourself to produce inspiring results.

We welcome you to this new relationship that we will create together. We hope you will enjoy our partnership as much as we have enjoyed creating the opportunity for it to be realized. This partnership encompasses the view of an effective leader as an individual who

Preface

can see through the fog of reality to interpret events and be able to make sense of the blurring and ambiguous complexity that engulfs us. To be able to do this has to do with having the best vision possible, generating trust, and knowing yourself, so that you can continue to learn and blossom. This leader needs to connect with people in their guts and in their hearts, and not just in their heads. Welcome to the leadership journey!

Acknowledgments

If we were to acknowledge all the leaders in our lives, the ones who inspired us to write about leadership and the ones who challenged us to be more than we were, we would have a list of names that would match this book in size, and then some. We could fill another volume with many students and colleagues from whom we have gathered ideas and with whom we have shared activities. Some of these women or men *are* named in the text. They are quoted and noted as their lives provide examples for the unfolding learning experiences presented here. Since we are not able to tell you of all our heroes and teachers in the time or space we have, we hope they know who they are and hope they will accept our thanks for their inspiration and teachings.

We want especially to thank our partners in life, Grace Gabe and Ken Cloke, for their love and light. Sidney Rittenberg and Betty and Monte Factor read early versions of the book and gave us valuable insights that we have incorporated. Near the very end of our revisions, Ken Cloke brought his loving editorial pen to our final draft. We thank him for contributing his elegant use of language to our efforts. Our assistants Lisa Miller, Grace Silva, Solange Raro, Anne Roswell, and Jubal Rafferty deserve special acknowledgment for doing what it took to produce this workbook. Thanks to our agent, Jim Stein, and our editor, John Bell. Their contributions made the process of bringing the workbook to publication smooth and satisfying. Finally we want to thank Miriam Goldsmith for her loving proofreading and much more.

Chapter 1

Leadership for a Successful Future

In which we establish the role of leadership in our future, draw the distinction between leaders and managers, assess our own leadership strengths, and create a personal leadership agenda.

We need leaders . . . who can situate themselves within a larger historical narrative of this country and world, who can grasp the complex dynamics of our peoplehood and imagine a future grounded in the best of our past, yet attuned to the frightening obstacles that now perplex us. Our ideals of freedom, democracy and equality must be invoked to invigorate all of us, especially the landless, propertyless and luckless. Only a visionary leadership that can motivate "the better angels of our nature," as Lincoln said, and activate possibilities for a freer, more efficient and stable America—only that leadership deserves cultivation and support.

Cornel West,
"Learning to Talk of Race," *New York Times Magazine,* August 2, 1992

The Future Is in Their Hands

The stakes for the leaders of our future are rising rapidly and daily. The demands on the role in both the public and private sector, the attention from the media to the problems we face, and the increased complexity of the world with globalization and galloping technology make leadership infinitely more difficult. The game has changed—dramatically. Strange new rules have appeared. The deck has been shuffled and jokers added.

Never before have American business, education, medicine, social welfare, and government faced so many challenges. There is a mood out there that must be termed dyspeptic—perhaps even murderous—toward institutional leaders. It's part of the American paranoid style. But it has been exacerbated by scandals, media attention, and questions about character. Uncertainties and complexities abound. There are too many ironies, polarities, confusions, contradictions, and ambivalences for any organization to understand fully. The only truly predictable thing right now is unpredictability. The new chic is chaos chic. Yogi Berra had it right, in his oft-quoted remark, that "the future ain't what it used to be."

The constancy of change, the challenge to reinvent government bureaucracy or corporate identity, the pressure to survive mergers and acquisitions, and the threat of failure through bankruptcy has led to hand-wringing and head-shaking in corporate board rooms, public agencies, and governmental offices. In traditional American institutions we've looked to the people who manage to save the day. But most of our managers came into being in a simpler time, when all they had to do to be successful was to build the best mousetraps and the world beat a path to their doors. Managers are not our saviors in this new environment. Constant change disturbs managers. It always has, and it always will. Machiavelli's observation that "change has no constituency" still rings true. In his book, *Adhocracy: The Power to Change,* Bob Waterman tells us that most of us are like the characters in Ibsen's play *Ghosts.* "We're controlled by ideas and norms that have outlived their usefulness, that are only ghosts but have as much influence on our behavior as they would if they were alive. The ideas of men like Henry Ford, Frederick Taylor, and Max Weber—these are the ghosts that haunt our halls of management."

Most of us grew up in organizations that were dominated by the thoughts and actions of the Fords, Taylors, and Webers, the fathers of the classic bureaucratic system. Bureaucracy was a splendid social invention in the nineteenth century, as the ideal mechanism for harnessing the manpower and resources of the Industrial Revolution. Today many organizations are reconsidering the macho, control-and-command mentality that is intrinsic to that increasingly threadbare model. They are looking to leadership that is empowering, that invites participation, that is flexible and responsive to the realities of life.

The Integrity of Leadership

As we begin, we must raise several cautions about leadership. First of all, leadership can be a heady experience. Learning about it, pursuing it, and encouraging it can take one on a dangerous power trip. If the purpose of leadership is, as we posit in this book, to take a stand for what one believes and to bring it forth into reality, then leaders must have a check on their ambition. In the leaders we admire, ambition is always balanced with competence and integrity. This three-legged stool upon which true leadership sits—ambition, competence, and integrity—must remain in balance if the leader is to be a constructive force in the organization rather than a destructive achiever of her or his own ends.

If the triad is out of balance and there is the formidable combination of ambition and competence, we are left with a self-serving leader who puts personal power above a vision for the good of the whole. The combination of integrity and ambition without competence can often lead to a well-meaning leader who is unable to make anything happen, taking the organization down a righteous dead end. Integrity paired with competence will often lead to good works but does not challenge barriers and open new ground. A three-way balance among these characteristics will enable a leader to be true to a vision beyond self and be able to make that vision real.

Second, leaders hold a sacred trust from their organization and its staff. Followers, who are often partners in an endeavor, look to leaders to interpret reality, explain the present, and paint a picture of the future. The awesome responsibility of finding the path for others and leading them on it requires that leaders remain in touch with the real world to avoid getting lost in a false image of themselves, a fantasy of their omnipotence and the addiction to power. A true leader uses reality as a tool for grounding the decisions he or she makes for others. Our good friend Sidney Rittenberg, China expert, business consultant, and author, describes the importance of information to a leader's role:

> Both a manager and a leader may know the business well. But the leader must know it better and in a different way. S/he must grasp the essential facts and the underlying forces that determine the past and present trends in the business, so that s/he can generate a vision and a strategy to bring about its future. One telling sign of a good leader is an honest attitude towards the facts, towards objective truth. A subjective leader obscures the facts for the sake of narrow self-interest, partisan interest or prejudice.

Effective leaders continually ask questions, probing all levels of the organization for information, testing their own perceptions, and rechecking the facts. They talk to their constituents. They want to know what is working and what is not. They keep an open mind for serendipity to bring them the knowledge they need to know what is true. An important source of information for this sort of leader is knowledge of the failures and mistakes that are being made in their organization.

Leaders, Not Managers

Given the nature and constancy of change and the challenges we face, the key to making the right choices will come from understanding and embodying the leadership qualities necessary to succeed in an increasingly volatile and mercurial global environment. To survive in the twenty-first century, we are going to need a new generation of leaders—leaders, not managers. The distinction is an important one. Leaders conquer the context—the turbulent, ambiguous surroundings that sometimes seem to conspire against us and will surely suffocate us if we let them—while managers surrender to it. Leaders investigate reality, taking in the pertinent factors and analyzing them carefully. On this basis they produce visions, concepts, plans, and programs. Managers adopt the truth from others and implement it without probing for the facts that reveal reality.

There is profound difference—a chasm—between leaders and managers. *A good manager does things right. A leader does the right things.* Doing the right things implies a goal, a direction, an objective, a vision, a dream, a path, a reach. Joseph Campbell, in a lecture given at Tarrytown Conference Center, New York, in 1985, cited the fact that lots of people spend their lives climbing a ladder—and then they get to the top of the wrong wall. Most losing organizations are over-managed and under-led. Their managers accomplish the wrong things beautifully and efficiently. They climb the wrong wall.

Managing is about efficiency. Leading is about effectiveness. Managing is about how. Leading is about what and why. Management is about systems, controls, procedures, policies, and structure. Leadership is about trust—about people.

Leadership is about innovating and initiating. Management is about copying, about managing the status quo. Leadership is creative, adaptive, and agile. Leadership looks at the horizon, not just the bottom line.

Leaders base their vision, their appeal to others, and their integrity on reality, on the facts, on a careful estimate of the forces at play, and on the trends and contradictions. They develop the means for changing the original balance of forces so that their vision can be realized.

A leader is someone who has the capacity to create a compelling vision that takes people to a new place, and to translate that vision into action. Leaders draw other people to them by enrolling them in their vision. What leaders do is inspire people, empower them. They pull rather than push.

This "pull" style of leadership attracts and energizes people to enroll in a vision of the future. It motivates people by helping them identify with the task and the goal rather than by rewarding or punishing them. Warren Bennis mentioned this in a lecture at AT&T not long ago, and a woman in the audience said, "I have a deaf daughter, so I've learned American Sign Language. In ASL, this is the sign for manage." She held out her hands as if she were holding onto the reins of a horse, or restraining something. She went on, "This is the ASL sign for lead." She cradled her arms and rocked them back and forth the way a parent would nurture a child.

Trust, Plus Vision, Plus Meaning

If you want to lead people, the first thing to do is to get them to buy into shared objectives. Then you have to learn how to generate and sustain trust. The trust factor is critical.

You must create an environment where people feel free to voice dissent. You do this through behavior. You do not fire people because they goofed, and you actually encourage dissent. You have to reward people for disagreeing, to reward innovation, and to tolerate failure. All these are connected with creating a trusting atmosphere—but most of trust comes not from a particular technique, but from the character of the leader.

In order to create trust, you need four ingredients. First, the leader has to have competence. The followers have to trust his or her capacity to do the job. One of the one hundred and fifty leaders interviewed for the book, *On Becoming a Leader,* was the director Sydney Pollack. One of the reasons people want to work with him is that he has a track record of Academy Award hits. They know he is competent at what he does.

Second, people are concerned with congruity—that the leader is a person of integrity. If you are an effective leader, what you say is congruent with what you do, and that is congruent with what you feel, and that in turn is congruent with your vision.

Third, people want a sense that the leader is on their side, that he or she will be constant. They want to know that in the heat of battle, their leader will support them, defend them and come through with what they need to win. Finally, if you are a leader who is trusted, you care about the lives of the people with whom you work, you empathize with them, and you care about the implications of your actions and the results of your decisions. Competence, congruity, and constancy, and caring—those are the qualities a leader must embody in order for trust to be created in a group. It takes a long time to generate and sustain. It takes repeated interactions.

The Buried Treasure

One of the interesting characteristics of successful leaders is the way they handle failure. The true leaders embrace error. We are not saying they want to fail, but that failure is not in their terminology. They might call it a "mistake," a "glitch," a "hash," a "miscue," a "false start," or a "misdirection." The word "failure" to most leaders connotes something that is terminal and lifeless.

Most of the people Warren Bennis interviewed for *On Becoming a Leader* looked forward to mistakes because they felt that someone who had not made a mistake had not been trying hard enough. Norman Lear, writer-producer at CEO Act III Productions, put it this way: "Wherever I trip is where the treasure lies." Katharine Graham, from the CEO Washington Post, said, "For me, a mistake is just another way of doing things."

These leaders, whatever walk of life they came from, whatever institution they presided over, always referred back to some failure—something that happened to them that was personally difficult, even traumatic, something that made them feel that desperate sense of hitting bottom—as something they thought was almost a necessity. It is as if at that moment the iron entered their soul; that moment created the resilience they needed. Real leaders keep the message moving; they make it clear to those they lead that there is no failure—only mistakes that give us feedback and tell us what to do next.

An Empowered Work Force

We have a basic ambivalence about authority in this country. We enshrine the myth of the lone hero, the outlaw, the renegade, the John Wayne cowboy, Gary Cooper in *High Noon*. The celebration of the self is deeply embedded in our culture. Our nation was founded by pioneers and by people who were oppressed and held leaders suspect. In our recent history there has been a lot of disappointment with leaders.

Some leaders do more harm than good. Have you ever worked for someone who made you nervous or a little crazy? A lot of stress and burnout has to do with bosses who communicate mixed messages. You're never sure where they're at. Or they are insecure and make your job impossible. There are all sorts of ways bosses can create problems. It's much like what doctors call iatrogenic disease: One of the unintended side effects of human intervention is to make people sick.

Proper leadership empowers the work force. An empowered work force is one that is committed, where workers feel they are learning, that they are competent. They have a sense of human bond, a sense of community, and a sense of meaning in their work. Even people who do not especially like each other feel the sense of community. A feeling of one's significance to others is extremely important.

Good leaders make people feel they are at the very heart of things, not at the periphery. Everyone feels he or she makes a difference to the success of the organization. When that happens, people feel centered and that gives their work meaning. Leadership gives the work force a sense of its own meaning, significance, competence, community, and commitment rather than compliance. It also gives work a sense of fun. It makes work something you look forward to, something pleasant. You get a kick out of work. Playwright Noël Coward once said, "Work should be more fun than fun."

Leadership Can Be Learned

Becoming a leader is not easy, just as becoming a doctor or a poet is not easy, and anyone who claims otherwise is fooling himself. But learning to lead is a lot easier than most of us think it is, because each of us possesses the capacity for leadership. In fact, every one of us can point to some leadership experience. Maybe the experience wasn't running a company or governing a state, but as Harlan Cleveland wrote:

> The aristocracy of achievement is numerous and pervasive. . . . They may
> be leaders in politics or business or agriculture or labor or law or education
> or journalism or religion or affirmative action or community housing, or
> any policy issue from abortion to the municipal zoo. . . . Their writ may
> run to community affairs, to national decisions or global issues, to a whole
> multinational industry or profession or to a narrower but deeper slice of
> life and work: a single firm, a local agency, or a neighborhood.
> (Harlan Cleveland, *The Knowledge Executive*)

He might have added a classroom, a union, a playground, and a political meeting to that list. Whatever your leadership experience has been, it is a good place to start. In fact, the process of becoming a leader is much the same as the process of becoming an integrated human being. For the leader, as for any integrated person, life itself is the career. Leadership is a metaphor for centeredness, congruity, and balance in one's life. Discussing the process in terms of "leaders" is merely one way of making it concrete.

The premise of this book is that leadership can be learned by each of us. More specifically, this book is about adult learning. Most psychologists have little to say about mental life or learning and growing in our adult years. For whatever reasons, we tend to associate creative behavior and learning with the young. It is probably a matter of socialization that we do not think of the mature (post-45, perhaps) as learners. The best information we have about what it takes to be a creative, generative adult suggests that we learn best when we are committed to taking charge of our own learning. Taking charge of our own learning is part of taking charge of our lives, which is the *sine qua non* of becoming an integrated person.

The act of committing oneself to being a life-long learner can take place at any point in our life. In this workbook, each of us has the opportunity to make that commitment and engage the learning process. No matter what your age, circumstances, or condition of life, the possibility of becoming a leader exists at every moment. This book is an invitation to begin now, if you have not already taken the first step.

Leadership talent can also be nurtured and developed at an early stage of life. John Gardner, former Secretary of Health, Education and Welfare and founder of Common Cause, addresses the question as it relates to the education of our youth:

> Can leadership be learned? . . . the notion that all the attributes of a leader are innate is demonstrably false. No doubt certain characteristics are genetically determined—level of energy, for example. But the individual's hereditary gifts, however notable, leave the issue of future leadership performance undecided, to be settled by the later events and influences.

> Young people with substantial native gifts for leadership often fail to achieve what is in them to achieve. So part of our task is to develop what is naturally there but in need of cultivation. Talent is one thing; its triumphant expression is quite another. Some talents express themselves freely and with little need for encouragement. Leopold Mozart did not have to struggle to uncover buried gifts in little Wolfgang. But, generally speaking, the maturing of any complex talent requires a happy combination of motivation, character, and opportunity. Most human talent remains undeveloped.

The Learning Plan of this Workbook

Gardner's observations about the waste of our leadership's potential serve as an indictment of our educational system and our experiences growing up. Because many of us have missed the opportunity to develop our leadership talents, we have a remedial task before us. It is now time to uncover our own and others' leadership abilities. We have written this book to support you in accomplishing this goal. We proposed a partnership with you in this endeavor. On our side, we agree to provide a program that will reveal the leadership abilities you may not have recognized in yourself, to hone the skills you may have blunted from lack of use, and to provide the encouragement that will inspire you to express yourself as the leader that you are. On your side of the partnership, we hope you will agree to take on this work with commitment, honesty, and a willingness to examine your basic assumptions about yourself and your life.

Chapter Two contains detailed instructions for using this workbook as a learning tool. In order to orient yourself to your qualities of leadership, we suggest you begin to develop your understanding of leadership with the activities below. The first distinction we would like to make is the one between leaders and managers. By focusing on this distinction, we better understand the need for leadership in our organizations.

The Distinctions between Managers and Leaders—An Exercise

Organizations need both managers and leaders to survive. However, in the future, definitions of success will be based on a new form of leadership. The old structure that exalted control, order, and predictability has given way to a nonhierarchical order in which all employees' contributions are solicited and acknowledged, and in which creativity is valued over blind loyalty. In the organization of the next millennium, vision, communication, innovation, flexibility, and inner directedness are prized. A new kind of leader has emerged, a leader who is a facilitator, not an autocrat; an appreciator of ideas, not a defender of them.

There is a profound difference between management and leadership, and both are important. "To manage" means "to bring about, to accomplish, to have charge of or responsibility for, to conduct." "Leading" is "influencing, guiding in direction, course, action, opinion." The distinction is crucial. As we said earlier, managers are people who do things right and leaders are people who do the right thing. The difference may be summarized as activities of vision and judgment—*effectiveness*—versus activities of mastering routines—*efficiency*. The chart below indicates key words that further make the distinction between the two functions:

Chart of Distinctions between Manager and Leader

The manager **administers**; the leader **innovates**.

The manager is a **copy**; the leader is an **original**.

The manager **maintains**; the leader **develops**.

The manager **accepts** reality; the leader **investigates** it.

Learning to Lead

The manager focuses on **systems and structure**; the leader focuses on **people**.

The manager relies on **control**; the leader inspires **trust**.

The manager has a **short-range view**; the leader has a **long-range perspective**.

The manager asks **how and when**; the leader ask **what and why**.

The manager has his or her eye always on **the bottom line**; the leader has his or her eye on the **horizon**.

The manager **imitates**; the leader **originates**.

The manager **accepts the status quo**; the leader **challenges it**.

The manager is the **classic good soldier**; the leader is his or her **own person**.

The manager **does things right**; the leader **does the right thing**.

....

....

....

....

Throughout this workbook we have created activities that will enable you to explore concepts about leadership and develop your leadership skills. In the following exercise we present an occasion for self-reflection and self-observation. We would like you to begin by completing this activity by yourself. In most cases, we will ask you to share your personal findings with colleagues. You may want to choose from among your responses the ones you would like to share with others. In all cases, we encourage you to be as honest with yourself as possible. Dip beneath the surface of your automatic reactions to discover your deeper concerns, perceptions, and wishes.

In the activities for this chapter, we first draw your attention to the distinction between leaders and managers, both in the abstract and then by thinking of specific colleagues in your life. Next, we ask you to create an agenda based on the distinction between managers and leaders for your learning experiences that can guide you as you use this workbook. We hope you will internalize the distinctions between these roles, and from this deeper understanding generate your own plan to become a leader.

The distinctions between leaders and managers drawn earlier are conceptual. They may be difficult to apply to your life without specific examples. In order to visualize clearly the distinction between manager and leader it is useful to picture people you know in these roles. Look to your own organization, corporation, agency, school, or primary identification group for people to consider. If you are a student and have not worked in an organization, choose your school, an informal organization to which you have belonged, a social group, or your family in order to perform the exercise.

1. Begin by making two lists. On the first chart, list the leaders in your organization or group and on the second, list the managers.

Examples of Leaders and Managers

LEADERS

	Name	Position
1.		
2.		
3.		
4.		
5.		
6.		
7.		
8.		

MANAGERS

	Name	Position
1.		
2.		
3.		
4.		
5.		
6.		

7.
. . . .

8.
. . . .

2. Given your list of managers and leaders, what other distinctions do you see that we may not have considered? Add them to the Chart of Distinctions on page 10. Expand this list to include additional characteristics of managers and leaders based on your experience with people you know.

3. Now, place your own name on the appropriate list as a leader or a manager.

4. Use the space provided below to answer to the following questions about the process of making your list and about the people on it:

Questions to Consider

A. Was it easier to identify managers or leaders in your organization or group? If so, which one and why?

. . . .

. . . .

. . . .

. . . .

B. Did you have more people in one category than the other? If so, which one and why?

. . . .

. . . .

. . . .

. . . .

C. Does your organization or group tend to support managers or leaders to a greater extent? Why?

. . . .

. . . .

. . . .

. . . .

D. If it does support one set of behaviors more than another, describe the ways it
    does this.

....

....

....

....

E. Where did you place yourself on the list? Why?

....

....

....

....

F. As you added new words to the Chart of Distinctions, did new names occur to
    you? If so, add them to the list.

The small group discussions in this workbook are intended to give you an opportunity to
test your perceptions against those of your colleagues. We assume that the wisdom of the
group is far greater than that of any individual. The give-and-take of these exchanges will
allow you to clarify your own ideas and learn from the diversity within your organization.
You may begin the discussion with our questions and then take it in new directions as
other topics emerge. In the process, you and your team of colleagues may discover new
aspects of leadership, you may learn about your lives in your organization, and you may
discover individual goals other than the ones we envisioned when writing this book. We
hope you do.

In order to expand your observations of the leaders and managers you know, find a partner
or a small group of associates with whom to share your perceptions. You may be in a
situation in which you do not have a small group available. You may be reading this book
on your own or using it in a large class with no small-group facilities. If so, create a study
group of your own that might include friends, your spouse, or classmates who may not be
reading the book but who are willing to discuss the questions with you.

Throughout the book you will be asked to work with others in the exercises. You may want
to establish a reference group with whom you work throughout the book on all the activi-

ties. If that is not possible, invite friends or colleagues to join you in the exercises that are most intriguing to you and for which you would like others' reactions, or add them to the agenda for the next staff meeting.

Activities to Consider

A. To begin with, present your revised Chart of Distinctions to others in the group. Come to a consensus on the distinctions you think are important. If you have differences of opinion, discuss them until you can reach alignment.

B. If there are several small groups that are discussing the Chart of Distinctions, share the chart from your small group with the others and see if you can come up with a complete list that represents the thinking of all groups.

C. Next, discuss the names each person has included on the chart of managers and leaders. In round-robin fashion, have each person share this list. How do the lists differ? Discuss the perceptions within the group.

D. Explain where you placed yourself and why. Ask the group for feedback. Did they place you in the same category? The group should give each person feedback regarding her/his own self-perception.

E. Next, discuss others on the list and come to a consensus regarding the characteristics of the managers and the leaders in your organization.

Your Leadership Assessment—An Exercise

From the previous exercise, you now have a beginning picture of the leaders and managers in your organization or group. How do you feel about your own and others' perceptions of your role? Did you receive any unusual feedback from your group? Do you see the ways in which your organization supports or detracts from leadership development? In this next activity, you will have an opportunity to clarify specific behaviors that you may want to change to become a more effective leader.

Our assumption in writing this book is that leaders are made, not born, and made more by themselves than by external means. No leader sets out to be a leader *per se,* but rather to express herself or himself freely and fully. That is, leaders have no interest in proving themselves, but an abiding interest in expressing themselves. The difference is crucial, for it is the difference between being driven, as too many people are today, and leading, as too few are.

To clarify the distinction between leader and manager, we have created an activity that will allow you to see where you fit on the continuum between leader and manager. The inventory contained in Tables 1 through 4 focuses on the characteristics, functions, philosophies, and results orientation of leaders and managers.

The inventory lists a group of characteristics of managing on the left side of each table and a group of characteristics of leading on the right side. In between is a scale on which you can assess yourself on these characteristics. On the scale, circle the number that best indicates your place on the spectrum between leader and manager. If, for example, you seek situations that are stable and guarantee prosperity more than situations that involve change, uncertainty, and growth, you would circle 1 or 2 for the first characteristic, depending on how often you seek these situations. If you favor neither situation you would circle 3. If, however, you are more drawn to change, uncertainty, and growth, you would circle 4 or 5. Think about how you usually function and circle the number that best represents your true thoughts and behavior. There are no right answers. This inventory will enable you to assess your leadership abilities as we move through the workbook. Refer to it as you work through the other exercises. As you develop new skills and begin to try out new behaviors, your agenda may change. Use this inventory again as a tool for measuring your growth.

Leadership Assessment Inventory—An Exercise

Table 1: Characteristic Differences between Leading and Managing

	Managing	Your Assessment	Leading
Seeks situations of	Stability Prosperity	1 2 3 4 5	Change Uncertainty
Focuses on goals of	Continuity Optimization of resources	1 2 3 4 5	Improvement Innovation
Bases power on	Position of authority	1 2 3 4 5	Personal influence

Demonstrates skills in	Technical
	  competence
	Supervision
	Administration
	Communication
		1 2 3 4 5	Diagnosis
			Conceptualization
			Persuasion
			Dealing with
			  ambiguity

Works toward outcome of	Employee compliance	1 2 3 4 5	Employee commitment

Table 2: Functional Differences between Leading and Managing

	Managing	Your Assessment	Leading
Planning strengths	Tactics Logistics Focus	1 2 3 4 5	Strategy Policy formation Seeing the big picture
Staffing approach	Selection based on qualifications	1 2 3 4 5	Training for positions Networks Developing shared values
Directing methods	Clarifying objectives Coordinating Establishing reward systems	1 2 3 4 5	Coaching Role modeling Inspiring
Controlling methods	Standard operating procedures Monitoring	1 2 3 4 5	Motivation Self-management Policy formation
Performance evaluation approach	Rewards Discipline	1 2 3 4 5	Support Development
Decision-making qualities	Analytical Risk-averse Rational	1 2 3 4 5	Intuitive Risk-taking Ambiguous
Communication style	Transactional Exchange Reciprocal	1 2 3 4 5	Transformational Committing people to action Persuasive

Table 3: Philosophical Differences between Leading and Managing

	Managing	Your Assessment	Leading
Oriented toward	Programs & procedures	1 2 3 4 5	People & concepts
Resources valued	Physical Fiscal Technological	1 2 3 4 5	People Informational
Information base of	Data, facts	1 2 3 4 5	Feelings, emotions, & ideas Things to learn
Human resources as	Assets to meet current organizational needs	1 2 3 4 5	Corporate resources for today & future development
Change attitude	Implements change by translating vision	1 2 3 4 5	Sees change as a raison d'être

Table 4: Expected Results of Management and Leading

	Managing	Your Assessment	Leading
Defines success as	Maintenance of quality Stability & consistency Efficiency	1 2 3 4 5	Employee commitment Mutuality/trust Effectiveness
Does not want to experience	Anarchy Employee disorientation Surprise	1 2 3 4 5	Inertia Lack of motivation Boredom
Is unsuccessful when experiencing	Deviation from authority Employee resistance Low performance	1 2 3 4 5	Consequences of selecting wrong direction/vision Failure to communicate vision Lack of buy-in

Share your assessment inventory with a partner who knows you and your role at work. Ask your associates for feedback on your perceptions of yourself. Is their view similar to yours? How does it differ?

Your Leadership Agenda—An Exercise

When you have completed the assessment inventory, review it to see if you circled a 3 or below on any item. If so, you are behaving more like a manager than a leader in this area. In order to express yourself more fully as a leader, we suggest that you create a personal agenda to guide you in transforming yourself. The following chart will enable you to build your leadership agenda. Using your inventory as a foundation, make a list of the behaviors you wish to change in the space provided. You can see from this list how you may wish to focus your attention as you read this book.

Share your agenda with your colleagues and friends and ask them for feedback. Can they support you in focusing on changing your behavior? If they have completed their own charts, compare their results with yours. Give them feedback as well. Are there common features to the agendas of your colleagues? If so, this may reveal biases and expectations in your organization. Notice similarities and differences in the analysis of barriers and supports. Similar perceptions of barriers among colleagues may indicate a pattern in the culture of the organization that limits the growth of leadership.

There may be many reasons why you are more involved with or identify more as a manager. These reasons can become barriers to developing your leadership potential. List them on your agenda as barriers along with other issues that block your emergence as a leader. We will say more about them in future chapters. For now, record them and then write the supports that can help you move closer to becoming a leader. We have provided an example of how to complete the Personal Leadership Agenda. In Chapter Two you will be asked to set goals for transforming yourself into a leader. The agenda you create here can serve as a foundation for you to revise as you become clearer about what you want to achieve and as you progress through the exercises.

Personal Leadership Agenda

BEHAVIORS I WISH TO CHANGE	BARRIERS	SUPPORTS
1. *Not strategic enough*	*Lack of information, lack of skills*	*Willingness to think strategically, team support*

2.

3.

4.

5.

6.

7.

8.

. . . .

. . . .

9. . . . .

. . . .

. . . .

10. . . . .

. . . .

. . . .

. . . .

In the next chapter we expand our repertoire of activities and exercises as we discover effective tools for transforming ourselves into leaders.

Chapter 2

How to Use This Workbook

In which we explore what this book will mean for our education as leaders, we begin the process of self-reflection and self-invention, and we commit to using this book as our tool for leadership transformation.

The best of all rulers is but a shadowy presence to his subjects.
Next comes the ruler they love and praise;
Next comes one they fear;
Next comes one with whom they take liberties . . .
Hesitant, the best does not utter words lightly.
When his task is accomplished and his work done
The people all say, "It happened to us naturally."

Lao Tzu, Tao Te Ching

The Reinvention of Self

We believe that leaders can be created by each of us—by ourselves and in community with one another. Right now, there are untold numbers of potential leaders in America—men and women full of passion for the promises of life, with no outlets for their passion. These undiscovered leaders have rich and powerful contributions to make to a society in desperate need of their talents. They are searching for the truth about themselves, a truth that will enable them to express their leadership voice. They are teachers who know how schools can be reformed, community activists who can redeem their troubled neighborhoods, health professionals who envision quality medical care for all, corporate staff members who are committed to an empowering workplace.

This workbook is written for those of you who want to find your own path to leadership. It is based on studies of established leaders conducted by Warren Bennis. His research, interviews, and first-hand observations provide a rich conceptual framework for learning. The activities and exercises in each chapter are based on Joan Goldsmith's experiences in educating young people and mature adults in the process of creating themselves as leaders.

Our experience shows that leaders are always originals, not copies. Because they find their own ways to express their leadership qualities, no one course will suffice for all leaders. This workbook provides multiple avenues for each person. Different starting points are honored. Different learning styles are encouraged. Different questions are considered.

Leaders, like all people, are the sum of all their experiences. But unlike many others, they amount to more than the sum, because they make more of their experiences. The problem with most leadership development programs is that they focus exclusively on skills—and although the skills can be useful, they are not enough. While the recent popularity of instant leadership courses is a symptom of a fundamental need for leadership, the courses themselves demonstrate our confusion about what constitutes leadership. Some claim it derives automatically from power. Others say it is mere mechanics—a thorough comprehension of the nature of organizations. Some say leaders are born, while others argue that they can be made, and according to the one-minute manager and/or microwave theory, made instantly. Pop in Mr. or Ms. Average, and out pops another McLeader in 60 seconds. Meanwhile, the need for leadership continues.

We are introducing a different path to leadership development—one that has twists and turns. It may not take the reader on a direct route to a finite end-place. We are suggesting an ambiguous process that begins and ends with self. What we are really talking about is becoming a leader through self-invention, through imagination. Inventing oneself is the opposite of accepting the roles we are brought up to play.

To be authentic is literally to be your own author (the words derive from the same Greek root), to discover your native energies and desires, and then find your own way of acting on them. When you have done that, you are not existing simply to live up to an image posited by the culture or by family tradition or some other authority. When you write your own life, you have played the game that was natural for you to play. You have kept covenant with your own promise.

Leadership of Your Own Life

We begin with the assumption that leaders are people who are able to express themselves fully. By this we mean that they know who they are, what their strengths and weaknesses are, and how fully to deploy their strengths and compensate for their weaknesses. They also know what they want, why they want it, and how to communicate what they want to others in order to gain their cooperation and support. Finally, they know how to achieve their goals. The key to full self-expression is understanding one's self and the world, and the key to understanding is learning—from one's own life and experience. The exercises in this book allow you to reflect on your self-expression and the internal processes that generate who you are in the world. We will support you in fully expressing yourself as a leader.

In this book we borrow stories about leaders from Warren Bennis's book *On Becoming a Leader.* We are interested not in theories about leaders, but rather in leaders functioning in the real world, not in some artificial setting—leaders whose lives have made a difference. They are thoughtful, articulate, and reflective. These leaders are by no means ordinary people. They work on the frontier where tomorrow is taking shape. As diverse as they are in background, age, occupations, and accomplishments, they are in accord on two basic points.

First, they all agree that leaders are made, not born, and made more by themselves than by any external means. Second, each of these individuals has continued to grow and develop throughout life. This is in the best tradition of leadership—people such as George Bernard Shaw, Margaret Mead, Charles Darwin, Eleanor Roosevelt, Nelson Mandela, Mahatma Gandhi, Golda Meier, Jean Piaget, and Martha Graham are a few examples that spring immediately to mind.

Germaine Greer, in her book *The Change,* creates a liberating vision for women over 50 who have experienced their biological change and with it the opportunity to transform many other aspects of their lives. She describes this later-in-life learning potential by pointing to some powerful role models:

> . . . if we look about us we can find examples of female recognition of a change: Josephine Baker began adopting children, when? When she was fifty. Nina Berberova left the Soviet Union for a new life, when? When she was fifty. When did Helen Deutsch leave Vienna? When she was fifty, with half her life still to live, for she died at the age of ninety-seven. Few

women devise as drastic a ceremonial as Helen Thayer, who at fifty-two "skied to the magnetic North Pole with her dog. She pulled a 160-pound sled for twenty-seven days and 345 miles, surviving seven polar bear confrontations, three blizzards, near starvation and several days of blindness." Thayer courted annihilation, and several times must have thought she had found it; she emerged reborn.

Thus, our message to you is that it is never too late to begin the process. Wherever you are in the midst of your life, now is the time to begin your own transformation. Something led you to this book. It may be a feeling inside yourself, a recognition that there is something you can contribute to yourself and others. We welcome the opportunity to work with you and hope you use it well.

The Inner Voice

Abbie Hoffman titled one of his early books *Steal This Book* to send a clear signal that he wanted the ideas put to work in making change in the society of the 1960s. We considered *Use This Book* as a title for our workbook because we hope you will make it your own, take it as your guide to create yourself as a leader.

Although everyone has the capacity for leadership, we do not believe that everyone will become a leader, especially given the confusing and often antagonistic context in which we now live. Too many people are mere products of their context, lacking the will to change or develop their potential. However, every person, of any age and in any circumstance, can transform themselves. Becoming the kind of person who is a leader is the ultimate act of free will; and if you have the will, this is the way.

First, use this as your workbook. Put your name on it. Write your thoughts and reactions on the charts and diagrams. Make notes in the margins. Have it document your journey to reinvent yourself as a leader. What we are suggesting is an introspective process. It requires being honest with yourself. We ask you to take a look inside. One of the leaders who understands this process is the television writer and producer, Norman Lear. He describes beginning this way: "First and foremost, find out what it is you're about, and be that. Be what you are, and don't lose it. . . . It's very hard to be who we are, because it doesn't seem to be what anyone wants." But, as Lear has demonstrated, it's the only way to truly fly.

So we begin with who we truly are, creating an internal dialogue to learn from ourselves. We will ask you to listen to your inner voice and to learn from the self who expresses itself as a leader. We also provide an opportunity to learn from colleagues and friends. The exercises are available for you to engage on your own and explore with others in small or large groups.

If you engage this learning process in an organizational environment, your growth will contribute to the future of the organization. Leaders are not made by theoretical course work any more than they are made by reading or studying: they grow by testing behavior in their work and in their lives. Education can provide awareness and stimulate individual development. However, if you are to have a lasting impact outside of yourself, your organization will need to support you by committing to learning opportunities, and by creating an environment for growth. Organizations tend to pay lip service to leadership development, but a study done by Lyman Porter and Lawrence McKibbon showed that only 10 percent of the companies surveyed devoted any time to it. For our society to grow the leadership to address the crises of our time, institutions must become learning environments for leadership. In this book we propose a number of ways in which organizations can stimulate this learning.

If you are a student engaging this book as part of your studies, you may want to use your experiences in school, in your family, and in your social group as reference points. It may be that your situation does not readily support opportunities for collaboration with colleagues on the exercises. If not, ask a friend or a roommate to be your partner. The value of the activities in the book is enhanced if you are able to share your insights and reactions.

The development of leaders begins and ends with you, the person who can reach inside, take hold of your desire to lead and commit yourself to noble purposes. Norman Lear describes four steps he took to develop himself as a leader. They were: become self-expressive, listen to one's inner voice, learn from the right mentors, and give oneself over to a guiding vision.

He goes on to tell of how he was profoundly influenced by Ralph Waldo Emerson's essay "Self-Reliance" in high school:

> Emerson talks about listening to that inner voice and going with it, against all voices to the contrary. I don't know when I started to understand that there was something divine about that inner voice. . . . To go with that— which I confess I don't do all of the time—is the purest, truest thing we have. And when we forgo our own thoughts and opinions, they end up coming back to us from the mouths of others. They come back with an alien majesty. . . . When I've been most effective, I've listened to that inner voice.

Self-Reflection

The process of reinventing yourself as a leader begins with an internal focus. Whether you realize it or not, you already have the ability, the knowledge, and the experience to become a leader. It will take becoming aware of your insights and practicing the effective behaviors that express your leadership talents. We have provided the framework of ideas and the enabling activities. The rest is up to you.

We start with reflection. Reflection not only on ideas but also on feelings. In the reflection process we include both the intellectual and emotional realities of our lives. We focus on the patterns of behavior that take us in a certain direction and are a result not only of what and how we think, but what and how we feel. Reflection is a pivotal way to learn about the choices and decisions we have made based on our experiences. By reflecting on the past and observing ourselves in the present, we begin to see the decisions we make as a result of the circumstances of our lives. These decisions about ourselves and about our world shape our stance toward leadership.

Consider some of the ways of reflecting: remembering back to earlier times; dreaming and letting your subconscious mind imagine; writing in a private journal; talking things over with someone you trust; watching yourself with your third eye; and hearing yourself in a new way. Reflection can take you to the heart of the matter, the truth of things. Often after appropriate reflection, the meaning of the past is known and the resolution of an incomplete experience becomes clear. By building on this completion you allow yourself to be expressive in new ways, to transform yourself into a leader. In the present, reflection allows us to choose a course of action that strengthens our expression leadership.

Throughout this book we pose questions that introduce the process of reflection and observation. We suggest that sharing the results of your reflections with others will deepen the process and allow you to connect yourself to your intentions. We also suggest actions you may take to revise your patterns of thinking, feeling, and behaving. As you work through the activities, other exercises may occur to you. You may develop additional questions to pursue. You may want to follow a different direction than the one we suggest. Go ahead and follow your own lead. We hope to create a beginning. Ultimately, becoming a leader is a personal process of transformation. You must choose your own way of getting there.

Personal Values for Effective Leaders—An Exercise

In the first chapter you created an agenda for yourself that included characteristics, functions, philosophical perspectives, and behaviors that can enable you to transform yourself from manager to leader.

In the activity below we ask you to reflect on your values, to focus on what is important to you in your life. Out of these values we ask you to create your own goals for achieving your transformation. Goals are end results. You will know when you have achieved a goal. It is a real accomplishment. Goals can often be created by projecting yourself forward in your life one, two, or three years and seeing what you would like to have accomplished by then.

Goals grow out of our values in life. We are motivated to achieve results that express our values and demonstrate what is important to us in the world. For Mathilde Krim, scientist for AIDS research, values express personal commitments. She reflects, "A value system, beliefs, are important so you know where you stand, but they must be your own values, not someone else's."

We have identified five values that are held by many of the leaders with whom we have interacted. These values express themselves in the actions, the commitments, and the concrete, tangible accomplishments of these leaders. There are many others we might have included. You may want to add others to the list for yourself. Effective leaders value clear communication, ethical practices, a diverse work force, on-going recognition, and participatory empowerment. As you review these values below, you may find that you feel strongly about some and are less committed to others. The goals you generate from these values will enable you to strengthen these values for yourself and thus increase your leadership effectiveness. There are several steps to the value/goal exercise:

1. Begin by returning to your Personal Leadership Agenda on page 18 and use the items in it as the basis for your thinking.

2. After you have reviewed your Personal Leadership Agenda, read the descriptions of the leadership values below and determine which values you hold strongly and which are less important to you. You may find that the values listed are all strong values for you. You may see that you have other values you wish to add to the list.

3. Next, determine the goals that are concrete expressions of each of your values. Consider what you need to accomplish to become a leader. Why have you become involved in this leadership project in the first place? In this exercise you will be most effective if you can be specific about what you would like to achieve.

4. The activity requires recognizing your values, stating what you intend to achieve, and referring back to these goals or objectives on a regular basis. In

this way you will be able to track your own progress. Goals that are realistic as well as inspiring will guide your future work. These goals can be the basis for your decisions about new ways of thinking and behaving.

We have suggested five values that, if held and expressed, will enable you to become a more effective leader. In the exercise below, evaluate the strength of the value, then answer the questions regarding goals related to each value. Remember to consider your Personal Leadership Agenda from Chapter One. For example, if you are working on the value of clear communication, look at your agenda items regarding directing and controlling, and notice if clear communication is a strong value for you. You might want to set goals that include becoming a coach for at least one other person within the next year, creating a mentoring program in your department within the next year, or taking new risks in communicating honestly with your supervisor in the next three months. If you answer the questions honestly, your goals will emerge.

Leadership Values

1. The Value of Clear Communication

Leadership calls for clear communication about goals, performance, expectations, and feedback. There is a value placed on openness and directness. Through effective communication, leaders support individual and team achievement by creating explicit guidelines for accomplishing results and for career advancement.

Strong Value   1   2   3   4   5   Weak Value

Questions to Consider to Generate Goals

A. How can I be clearer about my expectations of others' performance?

....

....

....

....

B. What guidelines for results do I need to establish and communicate?

....

....

. . . .

. . . .

C. What are my goals for communicating more effectively?

. . . .

. . . .

. . . .

. . . .

2. The Value of Ethical Practices

Leadership demands commitment to and demonstration of ethical practices. Creating standards for ethical behavior for oneself and living by these standards, as well as rewarding those who exemplify these practices, are responsibilities of leaders.

Strong Value   1   2   3   4   5   **Weak Value**

Questions to Consider to Generate Goals

A. What are my goals for becoming more aware of my own ethical principles and for demonstrating them in practice?

. . . .

. . . .

. . . .

. . . .

B. What are the ethics of my organization? How can I improve and reinforce them?

. . . .

. . . .

. . . .

. . . .

C. What are my goals for supporting ethical behavior among my colleagues, team members, and others in my organization?

....

....

....

....

3. The Value of a Diverse Work Force

Leadership values a diverse work force (diverse in race, sex, ethnicity, age, experience, and perspective) at all levels of the organization. Leaders are committed to taking full advantage of the rich backgrounds and abilities of all people and to promoting a greater diversity in positions of influence and power. Differing points of view are sought, and diversity is valued and honesty is rewarded.

Strong Value   1   2   3   4   5   **Weak Value**

Questions to Consider to Generate Goals

A. What are my goals for increasing my capacity to value and work with diversity?

....

....

....

....

B. How can I encourage greater diversity in my organization in positions of influence and power?

....

....

....

....

C. What can I do to reward the expression of diverse points of view?

....

....

....

....

4. The Value of On-Going Recognition

Leadership provides appropriate and on-going recognition—both financial and psychic—for teams and individuals who contribute to the success of the endeavor. Leaders recognize their own contribution to problems and acknowledge their own mistakes. Leaders value those who create and innovate as well as those who continually support the day-to-day requirements of the organization.

Strong Value   1   2   3   4   5   **Weak Value**

Questions to Consider to Generate Goals

A. How can I more effectively recognize the achievements of others?

....

....

....

....

B. What are my goals for an equitable recognition system?

....

....

....

....

C. What shortcomings or mistakes should I acknowledge in myself?

....

....

....

....

5. The Value of Participatory Empowerment

Leadership prizes the participation of those most directly involved in producing results by increasing their authority and responsibility. Teamwork, trust, and regular feedback are encouraged. In stimulating and releasing the capacity of all people in the organization, leaders increase their satisfaction and empower them to be successful.

Strong Value   1   2   3   4   5   **Weak Value**

Questions to Consider to Generate Goals

A. How can I more effectively empower others?

....

....

....

....

B. How can I increase my capacity to transfer authority and responsibility to those directly involved?

....

....

....

....

C. What can I do to enable colleagues to empower themselves for greater satisfaction and success?

....

....

....

....

Reflecting on your values and generating your goals is a useful exercise. However, without the commitment to being true to your values and achieving your goals, you are only completing an exercise in a workbook. Commitment is the missing piece in the puzzle of success. Leaders are clear about their commitments and are willing to declare them and demonstrate them in their actions. Commitment is the fuel that drives leaders. It links them to their values, makes others respect them, and motivates them to achieve their goals. As you create your goals in the exercise below, choose ones to which you can genuinely and enthusiastically commit yourself. As you share them with others in your group, let them know the strength of your commitment to realize these goals.

Personal Goals for Leaders—An Exercise

In answering the questions above you have clarified your values and identified a number of changes you would like to make in your thinking and behavior in order to become more effective as a leader. Some of your goals can be achieved in the short term, even as you read this book. Others will take longer and remain with you through the years.

In any change process, it is important to distinguish between what you can accomplish immediately and what will be the basis for an on-going life process. For example, you may choose as a goal becoming more conscious of diverse perspectives—perspectives other than your own—and being more open to divergent viewpoints on a regular basis. That is a short-term goal. A goal that might take longer to achieve would be to change your communication patterns so that you are clearer and more direct in sharing your expectations with others and letting them know when you are disappointed.

In completing the following chart, you have the opportunity to distinguish your short-term and long-term goals. Notice that there is a request for a date by which you will have achieved your goal. Without a projected date for completion, a goal lacks the demand to be accomplished. Each section of the chart includes an example to guide you. Try to commit yourself to a time deadline as you set your goals. This chart is a reminder of how you intend to change your patterns. As you work through the book, you may want to refer back to it to clarify your direction. You might want to post a copy near your work space to remind yourself of your intentions. You may also want to revise the chart as you proceed.

Goals Chart

SHORT-TERM GOALS (DATE)	LONG-TERM GOALS (DATE)
New Behaviors	
Be more willing to volunteer for responsibilities—11/1/98	*Create a long-range vision—2/1/99*

....

....

Communication

Be more direct in making requests—11/1/98   *Better communicate my vision—3/1/99*

....

....

....

Ethical Management Practices

Be more scrupulous about the accuracy of my   *With my team, create ethical standards state-*
expense report—10/1/98   *ment for clients—2/1/99*

....

....

....

Diversity

Be more sensitive to the comfort of the opposite   *Encourage others who disagree with me to*
gender when telling jokes—10/1/98   *speak up—2/1/99*

....

....

....

Recognition

Acknowledge the good work of a colleague at   *Do an inventory of my own accomplishments*
least once a day—9/1/98   *and create ways to be acknowledged—3/1/99*

....

....

....

Empowerment

Look for opportunities to transfer authority to   *Create a plan for greater sharing of decision*
others—9/1/98   *making—4/1/99*

....

. . . .

. . . .

Other Goals

. . . .

. . . .

. . . .

. . . .

Group Leadership—An Exercise

If you are working with a partner, classmates, in a team, or with other colleagues, you may want to share your individual goals. It is often useful to hear others' plans for their leadership projects. You may want to make additions or changes in your own chart based on what your colleagues suggest. In some cases, you may have information on your chart that is too personal to show to anyone else. That is fine. You do not need to share everything that you wrote. If each person communicates at least one goal it will be useful to the others. You may also use this group discussion as an opportunity to gain feedback from those who know you well. Ask them for their reactions to these questions:

Questions to Consider

A. Are my goals realistic? Have I set myself up for failure? Am I aiming too low for myself? Can I achieve more than I have targeted?

. . . .

. . . .

. . . .

. . . .

B. Given what you know about me, are there other areas that I should target for development?

. . . .

. . . .

. . . .

. . . .

C. Have I set short-term goals that will take longer to achieve or long-term goals that I can tackle sooner?

....

....

....

....

Your group may want to create a chart showing the group's goals. Begin by identifying one or two goals for each person that will be supported by the group. If you work in proximity to one another, you can post the chart near everyone's work space. It might look as follows:

Group Leadership Goals

SHORT-TERM GOALS (DATE)	LONG-TERM GOALS (DATE)
Person A	
....	....
....	....
Person B	
....	....
....	....
Person C	
....	....
....	....

As you look at each person's goals, you may discover that some are held in common by everyone. These common goals can form a project for the group. For example, several people may have the short-term goal of increasing the times and ways individual achievements are acknowledged in the department. The group may take on this goal and work on it together, mounting an acknowledgment campaign and planning rewards, special lunches, employee-of-the-month announcements, etc.

You may want to discuss ways to track individual and group goals to record the progress of each person. If you do, set up a reporting system that will let everyone know the results for both the individuals and the group. If your organization has regular staff meetings or uses electronic mail or voice communications systems, you can create tracking mechanisms that make everyone aware of the progress being made so they can support one another's efforts. A buddy system will allow colleagues to encourage each other to achieve their desired results.

Qualities that Support Leadership Development—An Exercise

In Chapter Four you will have an opportunity to gain feedback on your specific leadership skills. The results of exercises in "knowing yourself" will enable you to see the areas for your potential growth. At this point in the process, we would like to suggest that you conduct a mini-self-assessment in order to make your goals more concrete and give direction to your thinking and actions. This self-assessment focuses on the qualities that will support you in learning to become a leader. Through the answers to the questions, you will begin to see your strengths and weaknesses and understand how to focus your learning activities to improve your leadership skills.

Questions to Consider

A. Given my goals for reinventing myself as a leader, what are the qualities that I bring that will enable me to be successful?

. . . .

. . . .

. . . .

. . . .

. . . .

. . . .

. . . .

B. What are the elements of my style, personality, and skills that will make learning to be a leader more difficult? What is it about me that tends to get in the way of being a successful leader?

. . . .

. . . .

. . . .

. . . .

. . . .

. . . .

. . . .

C. Remember a time in recent years (as an adult) when you learned a new skill, played a new role, or took on a new physical challenge. What talents did you draw upon? What was it about your thoughts, feelings, and actions that allowed you to be successful? What stood in your way?

. . . .

. . . .

. . . .

. . . .

. . . .

. . . .

. . . .

D. How did you undermine yourself, devalue yourself, or misjudge yourself? What did you draw upon to overcome the odds and succeed?

. . . .

. . . .

. . . .

. . . .

. . . .

. . . .

. . . .

If you are working with a group of colleagues, share the qualities that you believe will enable you to be a better leader, and those that stand in the way of reaching your goals.

Ask your colleagues for feedback on your behavior. What are their perceptions about your behavior? Incorporate their comments into your responses to the questions above.

After each person shares the qualities that have enabled her or him to learn, have the group create a composite of the specific qualities that were mentioned that could support members of your group in learning to become a leader.

Qualities that Support Learning to Become a Leader

1. ....

2. ....

3. ....

4. ....

5. ....

6. ....

7. ....

8. ....

As you examine the qualities above, consider the ways your group and the organization as a whole can encourage each person to express her- or himself as a leader.

Questions to Consider

A. How can we as a group or organization support these qualities in ourselves and others so that we can become more successful in developing leaders?

....

....

....

....

....

....

....

B. How can we support one another in developing our leadership skills?

....

....

....

....

....

....

....

C. In examining the qualities the group identified, what were the qualities that were mentioned by colleagues that I had not considered?

....

....

....

....

....

....

....

The work you have done here to clarify your goals and identify the qualities you bring to achieving them will be useful throughout this workbook. As you continue, you may want to refer back to your goals and your qualities. They are reminders of where you are headed and what resources you bring to help you get there.

Chapter 3

The Leadership Crisis

In which we establish the societal leadership crisis, explore our models of leadership, debunk leadership myths, and reveal the patterns from our past that have shaped our personal views of leadership.

I consider many adults (including myself) are or have been, more or less, in a hypnotic trance, induced in early infancy: we remain in this state until—when we dead awaken . . . we shall find that we have never lived.

R. D. Laing, *The Politics of the Family*

The Loss of Leaders

Where have all the leaders gone? Many of them are, like the flowers of the haunting folk song, "long time passing." Leaders we once respected are dead. FDR, who challenged a nation to rise above fear, is gone. Churchill, who demanded and got blood, sweat, and tears, is gone. Schweitzer, who inspired mankind with a reverence for life from the jungles of Lambaréné, is gone. Einstein, who gave us a sense of unity in infinity, of cosmic harmony, is gone. Gandhi, John and Robert Kennedy, Martin Luther King, Jr., Malcolm X—all were slain, almost in testimony of the mortal risk in telling us that we can be greater, better than we are.

Where have all the leaders gone? The leaders who remain are the struggling corporate chieftains, the university presidents, the city managers, the state governors, the big city

41

mayors, the local community activists, and the school superintendents. Leaders today sometimes appear to be an endangered species, caught in a whirl of events and circumstances beyond rational control.

In the last two decades, there has been a high turnover, an appalling mortality—both occupational and actuarial—among leaders. In the last several decades, the "shelf life" of college presidents and CEOs has been markedly reduced. In the 1950s, the average tenure for college presidents was over eleven years; today it's more like four years. In the same way, corporate chieftains' days at the top seem to be numbered from the moment they take office. Superintendents of big city school districts last two to three years, often citing health reasons for leaving. In our local communities, the burn-out factor discourages school, government, and neighborhood activists from sticking to it for the long haul.

There are over 250 million Americans, and we have tried for a couple of decades to get along without leaders. It has not worked very well. So let us admit it: we cannot function without leaders. Our quality of life depends on the quality of our leaders. Since no one else seems to be volunteering, it is up to you. If you have ever had dreams of leadership, now is the time, this is the place, and you are it. We need you.

There are three basic reasons why leaders are important. First, they are responsible for the effectiveness of organizations. The success or failure of all organizations, whether basketball teams, movie makers, or automobile manufacturers, rests on the perceived quality at the top. Even stock prices rise and fall according to the public perception of how good the leader is.

Second, the change and upheaval of the past years has left us with no place to hide. We need something like a trim-tab factor, a guiding purpose. Leaders fill that need.

Third, there is a pervasive, national concern about the integrity of our institutions. Wall Street was, not long ago, a place where a man's word was his bond. The recent investigations, revelations, and indictments have forced the industry to change the way it conducted business for 150 years. Cynicism poisons our environment.

To observe that times are changing is an understatement. "Leadership in a traditional United States company," argues R. B. Horton, CEO of BP America, "consisted of creating a management able to cope with competitors who all played with basically the same deck of economic cards." It was an American game. The competition was fierce but knowable.

Play your cards right and you could win. As we all know, the game changed and grew strange new rules. Never before have American institutions faced so many challenges, and never before have there been so many choices over how to face those challenges. Uncertainties and complexities abound. The only thing that is truly predictable is unpredictability.

Two hundred years ago, when the Founding Fathers gathered in Philadelphia to write the Constitution, America had a population of only three million, yet six world-class leaders, at least, were among the authors of that extraordinary document. Washington, Jefferson, Hamilton, Madison, Adams, and Franklin helped create America. Today, there are over 250 million Americans, and where are the leaders of quality?

As eighteenth-century America was notable for its geniuses, nineteenth-century America was notable for its adventurers, entrepreneurs, investors, scientists, and writers, the titans who made the industrial revolution, the explorers who opened up the West, the writers who defined us as a nation and as a people: Thomas Edison, Eli Whitney, Alexander Graham Bell, Lewis and Clark, Hawthorne, Melville, Whitman, and Twain. These men whose vision matched their audacity helped build America.

Twentieth-century America started to grow on the promise of the nineteenth, but something went terribly wrong. Since World War II, America has been notable for its bureaucrats and managers, its organization men, its wheeler dealers who have remade, and in some cases unmade, the institutions and organizations of America, in both the public and private sectors.

We emerged from World War II as the richest, most powerful nation on earth, but by the mid-1970s America had lost its edge, and the much-bruited American century was suddenly the Japanese century—in business, anyway. Our arrogance at being the victors of World War II trapped us into a slumber of complacency. We are only now waking up. It is anyone's guess whose century it is politically. America lost its edge because it lost its way. We forgot what we were here for.

Today, the people who can afford to are increasingly retreating into their own electronic castles, working at home and communicating with the world via computers, screening their calls on answering machines, ordering movies for their VCRs, takeout food for their microwave ovens, and trainers for their bodies, keeping the world at bay with advanced security systems. They refuse to acknowledge what is happening—and the costs of what is happening—to those who lack their resources. Trend spotters call this phenomenon "cocooning," but it looks more like terminal egocentricity.

Learning to Lead

A nation cannot survive without public virtue; it cannot progress without a common vision. America has not had a national sense of purpose since World War II, or among a large part of its population since the 1960s, when, in an unprecedented show of common cause, millions of Americans vehemently opposed government policies. Instead of changing its policies, however, the government went underground. The Iran-contra affair, like Watergate before it, was an effort to deceive the American people, not our enemies.

As the government went underground and the more affluent among us took to their electronic towers, an especially ugly breed of entrepreneurial parasite took over our inner cities, peddling crack not only to the underclass, but to the uneasy rich and the bored children of the middle class. Today, Americans spend more money annually on drugs than on oil. The land of the free and the home of the brave is the world's number one drug addict.

Where have all the leaders gone? They're out there pleading, trotting, temporizing, putting out fires, trying to avoid too much heat. They're peering at a landscape of bottom lines. They're money changers lost in a narrow orbit. They resign. They burn out. They decide not to run or serve. They're organizational Houdinis, surrounded by sharks or shackled in a water cage, always managing to escape, miraculously, to make more money via their escape clauses than they made in several years of work. They motivate people through fear, by following trends or by posing as advocates of "reality," which they cynically make up as they go along. They are leading characters in the dreamless society, given now almost exclusively to solo turns. Thus, precisely at the time when the trust and credibility of our alleged leaders are at an all-time low and when potential leaders feel most inhibited in exercising their gifts, America most needs leaders—because, of course, as the quality of leaders declines, the quantity of problems escalates. As a person cannot function without a brain, a society cannot function without leaders. And so the decline goes on.

The Leadership Crisis

If it is true that the present leadership crisis is pernicious and all-pervasive, why should we bother to concern ourselves with it, to label it, understand it, describe or characterize it? Why do we need to analyze the extent of the problem? What difference could it make in our daily lives if we were to comprehend better and become conscious of our potential for leadership?

In an earlier book, *Why Leaders Can't Lead,* Warren Bennis wrote that there is an uncon-scious conspiracy in our country to discourage and suppress genuine leadership. A wide-spread unspoken fear of the potentially negative consequences of creative leadership blankets our thoughts and actions. It prevents the most talented among us from talking boldly or expressing ourselves as leaders. This conspiracy is all-encompassing, lulling us into confor-mity, complacency, cynicism, and inaction. As a nation, as organizations and as individu-als, we fear taking risks. We do not expect ourselves or others to stand up and be counted, and become frightened when they do.

We are purposefully sounding an alarm when we refer to a conspiracy and a leadership *crisis* in our society. The first step in the process of becoming a leader is to wake up to the need for a new stance toward leadership. Without a clear sense of the problem, we do not know how to tackle it. It is our hope that by raising this issue we will stir *you* to becoming aware of and taking responsibility for our leadership challenge.

After we become aware of the barriers we face in expressing ourselves as leaders, we can transform ourselves into *responsible* leaders who can break this unconscious conspiracy and demonstrate the courage to solve the problems of our time. For those of you who are willing to begin to shape yourselves as leaders, we suggest a first step. It is to become conscious of the effects you have experienced in your own life of the lack of leadership.

Our culture consistently fails to support the growth and development of leadership. It is as difficult for us to be conscious of this culture as it is for a fish to be aware of the water in which it swims. We do not notice that we are being discouraged from exhibiting leadership qualities. The context of our work and personal lives reinforces a set of common values, attitudes, and perceptions that discourages us from standing out in a crowd, that calls for playing it safe.

The first step in becoming a leader, then, is to recognize the context for what it is—a breaker not a maker, a trap not a launching pad, an end not a beginning—and declare your independence from it.

Leaders from the Past—An Exercise

Our personal view of leadership is shaped by the experiences from our past. In part, we all make decisions about leadership based on what we have learned from our families or schools, from direct encounters with leaders we have known, or from observations of distant heroes.

Learning to Lead

We have created unconscious patterns and insights from these past experiences that now inform our actions. To the extent that we are unaware of these patterns or the context in which they arise, we are complicit in an unconscious conspiracy.

Who were our mentors? Who walked through our dreams? Who were the giants, larger than life, who inspired us to act? Who were the real people who made a difference in our lives? We are going to use this exercise to discover the hidden models we carry in our memories and our hearts of the women and men who shaped our expectations for ourselves.

The answers to these questions and your comments on the following chart will reveal the experiences that shaped your personal view of leadership. You will gain a view of the people you knew and the decisions you made as a result of how you saw their lives.

If you are working in a small group, complete the exercise as an individual, then compare and discuss your responses with your colleagues.

Leadership Models

1. Who were the leaders from your past whom you remember and revere? Whom do you consider a leader in your current life?

Questions to Consider

A. Name three people who walked through your dreams as heroes from the past.

....

....

....

B. Name three leaders you respect and value who are currently in your life.

....

....

....

2. What were the results of their leadership? How did their lives unfold? What happened to these leaders in their personal lives and on the larger stage of their work and accomplishments?

Questions to Consider

A. For each person from your past, indicate their successes and failures and your assessment of their achievements.

....

....

....

....

....

....

....

B. As you view current leaders, indicate the obstacles they face in expressing their leadership abilities and the rewards they gain from being leaders.

....

....

....

....

....

....

....

C. How would you assess these leaders in terms of the risks they took and the results they achieved? How would you sum up their lives?

....

....

....

....

....

....

....

....

3. What did you learn about leadership from these heroes? How did their personal characteristics, their view of life, and their actions have an impact on your vision of yourself?

Questions to Consider

A. As you operate in your life on a day-to-day basis, how do you use what you have learned from your heroes?

....

....

....

....

....

....

....

....

B. What positive and negative aspects of life and leadership did you learn from these men and women who shaped your view of leaders?

....

....

....

....

....
....
....
....

On the following chart, list six qualities, six attitudes, and six behaviors that characterize the leaders you remember and those you currently know. Indicate what you learned from these leaders that has been valuable in your personal and professional life. In creating this chart, look for the qualities, attitudes, and behaviors that are common to several individuals. Then summarize the leadership traits you have learned from these men and women who are your models.

Leadership Qualities, Attitudes, Behaviors, and Lessons Chart

QUALITIES	ATTITUDES	BEHAVIORS	LESSONS
1. *personal integrity*	*constructive*	*outspoken*	*speak your mind*
2.			
3.			
4.			
5.			
6.			
7.			

Learning to Lead

What can you learn from this chart? Probe beneath the surface comments to discover a deeper level of insight. Notice the patterns, decisions, and attitudes about leadership that have affected your life.

Questions to Consider

A. What inspiring and positive lessons about life and leadership can you draw from the experiences of others?

....

....

....

....

....

....

B. What negative messages did you receive from analyzing the lives of these women and men?

....

....

....

....

....

C. Given the qualities, attitudes, and behaviors of these leaders, what aspects of their lives had the greatest impact on your own life choices? Why were you particularly influenced by these qualities?

....

....

....

....

....

....

Working with a small group or with a colleague or partner, create a chart that is a synthesis of the qualities, attitudes, behaviors, and lessons identified by each person. In creating the synthesis chart, discuss the following questions:

Questions to Consider

A. How did the insights about leadership differ for each member of your group?

B. Were there disagreements among group members about the entries on the chart? If there were differences, discuss how each person viewed the qualities of leadership that influenced them.

C. Notice that the same qualities and messages may be interpreted by some group members as positive and by others as negative. If so, discuss what is behind these different points of view.

D. If you are working in a small group that is part of a larger collection of other groups, have one member of your group give a summary of the synthesis from your small group to the larger group. Compare similarities and differences across groups.

E. Notice the differences in leadership attributes as a result of position, role, organizational structure, length of time in the organization, etc.

Leadership Myths—An Exercise

One of the problems we face in recognizing leadership qualities and talents is that we are unaware of the myths about leaders that may be shaping our beliefs. Every culture, whether societal or organizational, creates myths that in turn influence our values, beliefs, and ways of thinking. The myths about leadership that operate in our culture tell us whom to acknowledge in leadership roles. When a culture idolizes anti-heroes, as ours has, it is a sign that the society is in trouble.

The leadership myths of our culture do not support the emergence of unorthodox leaders. Rather, they hinder self-expression unless it reinforces one of the prevailing myths. Belief in the myths and the need to perpetuate them keep us from taking risks as leaders. We would like you to become more aware of the influence of these myths on your thoughts and behavior, and have described some of them below. As you read them, try to imagine times when you heard or saw this myth being promulgated.

Questions to Consider

A. Who told you this myth was true?

B. Who demonstrates this myth? Who lives their life out of this myth?

C. Following the description of each myth, write the name of a person who reminds you of the myth.

D. In the space provided below each myth, describe an incident when you thought the myth was true or when people you knew believed in the myth and operated as if it was real.

Myths

1. Leadership Is a Rare Skill

Nothing could be further from the truth. While *great* leaders may be as rare as great runners, great actors, or great painters, everyone has leadership potential. There are millions of leadership roles throughout the country. People may be leaders in one organization and have quite ordinary roles in another. We know of a clerk at J.C. Penney's who is a powerful leader of a church group and a retired beer salesman who is the mayor of a medium-sized town.

2. Leaders Are Born Not Made

Biographies of great leaders sometimes read as if they entered the world with an extraordinary genetic endowment, as if their future leadership role was preordained. Do not believe it. The truth is that major capacities and competencies of leadership can be learned if the basic desire to learn them exists.

This is not to suggest that it is easy to learn to be a leader. There is no simple formula, no rigorous science, no cookbook that leads inexorably to successful leadership. Instead it is a deeply human process, full of trial and error, victories and defeats, timing and happenstance, intuition and insight. As one leader put it, "It is not easy to learn how to lead. It's sort of like learning how to play the violin in public."

. . . .

. . . .

. . . .

. . . .

. . . .

. . . .

. . . .

3. Leaders Are Charismatic

Some are, but most are not. Leaders, for the most part, are "all too human." They are short and tall, articulate and inarticulate, dress for success and dress for failure, and there is nothing in terms of appearance, personality, or style that sets them apart from their follow-ers. Our guess is that charisma is rather the result of effective leadership, and those who master it are granted respect and even awe by their followers, increasing the attraction between them.

. . . .

. . . .

. . . .

. . . .

. . . .

. . . .

. . . .

. . . .

4. Leadership Exists Only at the Top of an Organization

We may play into this myth by looking to the executives of large organizations for examples of leaders, but it is obviously false. In fact, the larger the organization, the more leadership roles it is likely to offer. General Motors has thousands of leadership roles available to employees, as does the United Auto Workers, its counterpart union. Many large organizations are creating more leadership roles through self-directed teams, shared decision making, and the creation of small entrepreneurial units within the organization that have the freedom to operate virtually as independent businesses.

. . . .

. . . .

. . . .

. . . .

. . . .

. . . .

. . . .

5. The Leader Controls, Directs, Prods, Manipulates Others

This is perhaps the most damaging myth of all. Leadership is not so much the exercise of power as the empowerment of others. Leaders lead by pulling rather than by pushing; by creating achievable, challenging expectations and rewarding progress toward them, rather than by manipulating; by enabling people to use their own initiative.

. . . .

. . . .

. . . .

. . . .

. . . .

. . . .

. . . .

6. Other Myths

Do you have other myths, misconceptions, and beliefs about leadership? Please add them to the list and share them with colleagues. If you are working in a small group, create a list of the myths that are common to your organization.

. . . .

. . . .

....

....

....

....

....

....

....

Questions to Consider

A. If you were able to identify individuals or incidents that exemplified a myth, state why the myth seemed to be true. What purpose does it serve? What was required from everyone else to reinforce the myth and perpetuate it?

....

....

....

....

....

....

....

....

B. What are the leadership myths in your organization? How does your organization propagate its leadership myths?

....

....

....

....

....

....

....

....

C. How do the leadership myths in your life influence your behavior and your self-assessment?

....

....

....

....

....

....

....

D. How do your position, role, and responsibilities in the organization shape your myths about leadership?

....

....

....

....

....

....

The Leadership Gap—An Exercise

Every day we encounter situations, circumstances, or seemingly impossible problems that could be ameliorated if not solved by the exercise of leadership. Often we are unaware that leadership is needed. Unseeing, we do not act ourselves, nor do we empower others to fill the void. Our belief in leadership myths blinds us to our hidden potential for responding. In an almost unconscious state, we do not recognize that leaders can make a difference. We feel unsettled. We have a nagging feeling that something is unexpressed. There is an uncomfortableness, a "dis-ease" with the flow of events and results that seem inevitable.

In the next exercise we will increase our awareness of the times and places when leadership might have made a difference, when it could have had an impact on the events in our lives. By noticing when leadership was required, where leadership is missing, and how the leadership gap occurred, we can begin to respond with the thoughts and actions that might change our own world and the lives of others.

We begin by focusing our attention on the need for leadership in the larger community. To remind yourself of scenarios that might require leadership, review local and national newspapers, news magazines, and other publications to identify stories about problems that are at impasse and do not seem to have a resolution. Examples have been provided for each part of the exercise.

Questions to Consider

A. Create a list of situations that seem to be in turmoil or at impasse and that might be moved forward or resolved by the intervention of a leader. Look for at least five situations.

1. *Conflict over use of public parks by people who are homeless.*
....

....

....

2. ....

....

....

3. ....

....

....

4.
....

....

....

5.
....

....

....

6.
....

....

....

7.
....

....

....

C. Create a scenario for each situation that describes how it might be improved by the intervention of a leader.

1. *A leader is needed who can listen to both sides and propose a model for a problem-solving session in which both sides come together and mediate a solution.*
....

2.
....

3.
....

4.
....

5.
....

6.
....

7.
....

D. What keeps you from taking the action you know is needed to solve the problem? What leadership myths obstruct your view? What supports you in demonstrating leadership in this situation?

I have a fear of rejection and the feeling that I am at the bottom of the hierarchy with no power. I am blocked by the myth that leadership exists only at the top. I am supported by friends who look to me for solutions and appreciate my interventions.

....
....
....
....
....
....
....

E. What would you do to solve the problem? How would you demonstrate leadership ability?

I would ask each side to meet with me and would begin by listening to their points of view. I would then ask them to meet together and try to create a common vision with them of the problem. I would then work with them to come up with a solution that meets both sets of needs and supports the common vision.

....
....
....
....
....
....
....

Learning to Lead

In a small group, or with a partner at home, discuss one particular problem situation that you or a member of the group has identified. Assume you are a group of consultants to a leader who must grapple with the situation. Come to consensus on the advice you will give him or her and describe the advice below.

....
....
....
....
....
....
....
....
....

In giving your advice, pay attention to the ethical considerations of the situation and the personal abilities and personal agenda of the leader.

Leaders in Our Families—An Exercise

Many of us can make the charge that Franz Kafka so eloquently directs in his *Diaries* to the adults who shaped his childhood:

> When I think about it, I must say that my education has done me great harm in some respects. This reproach applies to a multitude of people— that is to say, my parents, several relatives, individuals, visitors to my house, various writers, a crowd of teachers—a school inspector, slowly walking passers-by; in short, this reproach twists through society like a dagger. . . . I can prove any time that my education tried to make another person out of me than the one I became.
>
> (Franz Kafka, *Diaries 1910–1931*)

For the most part, schools and families have failed to create a nurturing and supportive context for our development as leaders. As long as this context, which is inherited from our youth and shapes our current view of ourselves, remains invisible to us, we cannot shift our thinking or our behavior to fill the leadership gap. Before we can learn to lead, we must learn about the context that limits the full expression of leadership. Indeed, anyone who does not master the context will be mastered by it. In this exercise we conduct an analysis of the context that was created closest to home, in our families.

We begin with our families of origin, the ones in which we grew up. They are the most powerful learning environments we will experience in our lives. It is in the family that we first develop a sense of our own identity, our values, our aspirations, and our expectations for life. It is in our families that we have the least examined and the most determining experiences. Because our family life was so powerful in influencing our views of leadership, and because we often maintain an unconscious barrier to recognizing its impact, it is difficult to uncover the lessons we learned and the messages we received.

Begin the exercise with interviews of your family members. If you are fortunate enough to have members of an older generation still living, you can start this exercise with them. If not, talk to other members of your family of origin. If you are the sole member of your family, plumb your own memories. Try to discover answers to the following questions:

Questions to Consider

A. Who were considered leaders in your family? Who were the heroes and heroines? For what traits? Make a list and notice who is included and who is excluded. Ask several family members the same question and compare their responses. Who showed up on all the lists? Who did not appear on the lists of others but are people you would include on your list?

....

....

....

....

....

....

....

....

Learning to Lead

B. How did your family view leadership? Was it something far off in the distance that only "great men" exhibited? Were there leaders of both genders right at home? How was leadership defined?

....

....

....

....

....

....

....

....

C. Were leaders identified with a particular gender, a particular place in the sibling hierarchy, a special branch of the family, a particular culture or race?

....

....

....

....

....

....

....

....

D. What were the signals sent to you about being a leader? Who sent them and how were they delivered? Was the communication subtle or direct? How did you respond? Did you rebel or did you conform?

....

....

....

....

. . . .

. . . .

. . . .

. . . .

E. How were you encouraged or discouraged to exercise your leadership skills?

. . . .

. . . .

. . . .

. . . .

. . . .

. . . .

. . . .

. . . .

If you are able to work on this exercise in a small group, compare notes and exchange anecdotes. Notice the variety of responses from different families. As a group, collect common themes, insights, and conclusions. What are the different attitudes toward leadership expressed in different families? How did culture, ethnicity, immigration, and social class influence leadership patterns? If you are part of a larger session, you may want to communicate your findings to the other groups. As you exchange your observations you may find that your family's contribution to your view of leadership and yourself will emerge.

We will now create a family tree that diagrams the history of leadership for generations past. There are many approaches to genealogical research and family trees available. We have created the leadership family tree on page 65 for you to use to diagram your family's history in relation to leadership. In this exercise, we invite you to use the diagram filling in the information for your ancestors, going back as many generations as you can. By creating your family tree, you can see the legacy, the models, and the messages that have been passed down to you through the generations. You will see, in bold relief, your family members' participation in leadership roles. You will discover the ones they assumed and those they did not. Knowledge of our family's history allows each of us to be more conscious of the choices available to us. Susan Griffin, in her extraordinary work *A Chorus of Stones,* writes about the power of revealing our family's history to ourselves:

> I am beginning to believe that we know everything, that all history, in-
> cluding the history of each family, is part of us, such that, when we hear
> any secret revealed, a secret about a grandfather, or an uncle, . . . our
> lives are made suddenly clearer to us, as the unnatural heaviness of unspo-
> ken truth is dispersed. For perhaps we are like stones; our own history and
> the history of the world embedded in us, we hold a sorrow deep within
> and cannot weep until that history is sung.

The leadership roles you enter on the chart may come from all parts of life: church, family, school, community, work, and the larger world. Include any expression of leadership that you can remember or discover in your family history. You may also want to ask your spouse or partner to complete a similar chart and compare notes with yours. Notice the patterns you each inherited. Observe how you carry these patterns into your work environment. Do you notice any parallels? When you have completed the chart, show it to a family member and discuss your observations. It is through these conversations that our "history is sung" and that we are released from the hold of unconscious patterns from the past.

In each box in the chart, list the name of the person and the leadership role they played. You may want to use one color for you and your direct ancestors, and another color for other members of your family.

Leaders in Our Organization—An Exercise

We carry our family patterns with us to work. They are reshaped, revised, and revisited as we interact with the values, culture, and expectations of the organizations that house us in our adult lives. We learn about leadership from our colleagues in these organizations, and we also learn from the structures and systems of the institutions themselves.

Take a dispassionate look at your place of work, the environment in which you spend the majority of your waking hours. How are leaders viewed, rewarded, and developed? How are they discouraged or punished? What has been the impact of their implicit and explicit messages on your vision of yourself and your role as a leader? We begin the exercise below by analyzing the organization in which you currently work. You may want to observe other institutions you have known in the past.

Complete the following chart, indicating the ways your work environment supports the expression of leadership on an ongoing basis and the ways it discourages the development of new leadership. Also note that organizations express their support or discouragement of leadership through explicit rewards, promotions and acknowledgment. Other, more subtle means of signaling attitudes toward leadership—such as training programs, social patterns,

Leadership Family Tree

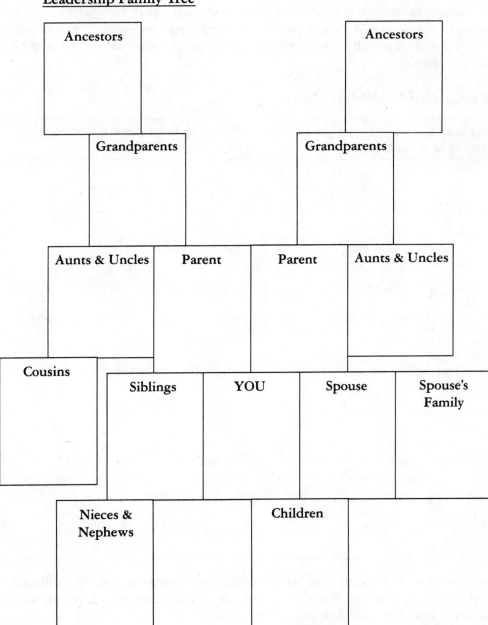

values, communication systems, and staff structures—are also employed. In some organizations that are introducing self-managing teams or nonhierarchical work groups, leadership may not be associated with title or position. In completing this exercise you will want to observe the hidden as well as the explicit signals, and the traditional as well as the new forms of leadership.

Organizational Leadership Chart

Ways my Organization Supports Expressions of Leadership	Ways my Organization Obstructs Expressions of Leadership
....	....
....	....
....	....
....	....
....	....
....	....

If you are alone in analyzing your work environment, show your chart to a colleague or friend who knows your work situation for feedback on your perceptions. If you are working in a group, have each individual complete the chart.

Activities to Consider

A. Compare charts and discuss the differences and similarities.

B. Discuss specific examples of situations that have supported or obstructed leadership in your experience.

C. Have your group come to consensus on the supports and obstacles to leadership, then complete a group chart that shows this consensus.

D. If you are in a larger session, present your group chart to the other groups. Discuss the common factors and explain the underlying dynamics that produce them.

As you work in the environment you have described above, take a look at how it has influenced the choices you have made. What has been the impact on your behavior? How has it shaped your expression of yourself? Who are the colleagues you respect and emulate? When have you stood up to be counted? When have you held back from playing a leadership role?

Questions to Consider

If you are working alone, describe two scenarios for yourself: one in which you played a leadership role at work, and one in which you avoided being a leader. For each scenario identify the following:

A. The patterns I've discovered from my family history that block or support me as a leader:

....

....

....

....

B. Messages I have received from my work environment that have encouraged or discouraged me as a leader:

....

....

....

....

C. Comfort or discomfort I felt in playing the role of leader:

....

....

....

....

....

D. Rewards or punishments I received for my behavior:

....

....

....

....

....

E. Decisions I made as a result of my behavior and/or the response of others:

....

....

....

....

....

After you have answered these questions you may want to share your responses with a colleague. You may want to reflect on the work you have done in this chapter to understand the leadership crisis in our society and your personal relationship to it. If you notice any changes you would like to make in your own behavior, we encourage you to act on your insights. In the next chapter we will go more deeply into the process of understanding yourself and the role self-knowledge plays in becoming a leader.

Chapter 4

Knowing Yourself

In which we become aware of our inner voice, learn how we learn, and shift our paradigm of leadership to include viewing failure as an opportunity for growth.

I have often thought that the best way to define a man's character would be to seek out the particular mental or moral attitude in which, when it came upon him, he felt himself most deeply and intensively active and alive. At such moments, there is a voice inside which speaks and says, "This is the real me."

William James, Letters of William James

The Beginning

Leaders know themselves; they know what they are good at doing. They apply their skills and competencies. Part of their secret is that they have a positive self-regard, they know their talents, they nurture them, and they are able to discern how what they are good at doing can help their organization.

It is an intense journey to achieve a positive sense of ourselves and know our abilities and our limitations. We get there by understanding what it takes for us to learn about ourselves, by being able to solicit and integrate feedback from others, by continually keeping ourselves open to new experiences and information, and by having the ability to hear our own voice and see our own actions.

69

Learning to Lead

Self-reflection is the first key to becoming a leader. When you reflect on your experiences, include everything from reviewing last week's calendar to looking at critical incidents in which you have been involved—both the successes and failures. It may mean keeping a journal. It may mean going on a sabbatical, as John Sculley does on a regular basis. We know a college president who takes a month sabbatical every year to reflect on her life and the life of the college. She is modeling her role as the leader of a community of learners. She demonstrates that the process of renewal and knowing oneself is a life-long process.

Interaction with others who will tell us about ourselves is the second source of information for knowing ourselves. It may mean soliciting feedback from valued friends and co-workers. Hearing "reflective backtalk" from friends, colleagues, spouses, and significant others allows us to "true" ourselves in relation to their perceptions. With this input we can integrate our internal conversations with data from the external world to enrich the process of knowing ourselves better.

Being continually open to learning is the third aspect of self-knowledge. Some people respond to change by getting all tied up in knots. They keep adhering to earlier scripts, using the same lecture notes, repeating the same mistakes. These people have forgotten how to learn. Remaining open to new learning means being truthful with ourselves and others, being willing to re-evaluate our prior beliefs in the face of new information that contradicts what we know to be true, and finally continuing to remember what is important—being clear about our priorities and our goals.

The fourth way we know ourselves has to do with the internal and external consistency of the self, knowing ourselves well enough for there to be a continual connection between what we believe and what we do and say. Having integrity, demonstrating wholeness, and being of one piece are all ways of expressing yourself. We find that Max DePree, CEO of Herman Miller Company, says it best in the moving prologue to his book *Leadership Jazz:*

> Esther, my wife, and I have a granddaughter named Zoe, the Greek word
> for "life." She was born prematurely and weighed one pound, seven ounces,
> so small that my wedding ring could slide up her arm to her shoulder.
> The neonatologist who first examined her told us that she had a 5 to 10
> percent chance of living three days.
>
> To complicate matters, Zoe's biological father had jumped ship the month
> before Zoe was born. Realizing this, a wise and caring nurse named Ruth

gave me my instructions. 'For the next several months, at least, you're the surrogate father. I want you to come to the hospital every day to visit Zoe, and when you come, I would like you to rub her body and her legs and arms with the tip of your finger. While you're caressing her, you should tell her over and over how much you love her, because she has to be able to connect your voice with your touch.'

Ruth was doing exactly the right thing on Zoe's behalf (and of course, on my behalf as well), and without realizing it she was giving me one of the best possible descriptions of the work of a leader. At the core of becoming a leader is the need always to connect one's voice and one's touch.

(Max DePree, *Leadership Jazz*)

We must be able to hear our own voice and realize the power of connecting it with our touch. If we have a clear awareness of who we are, we can develop the habit of staying tuned to what we say and do. In the following pages we will suggest ways of learning more about this process and how to develop the constancy that Max DePree was able to give Zoe as she brought herself to life.

The Shift in the Leadership Paradigm

"Paradigm" has become a trendy word in social science literature in recent years. The popularity of the concept probably stems from the realization that our current way of thinking, of seeing the world, and of interpreting the data that we encounter is not effective in producing the results we hope to achieve. We not only need new ideas, we need a new *way* of thinking. In order to transform ourselves as leaders, we must recognize and then shift the paradigm through which we view leadership itself.

A paradigm is a framework, a construct, a contextual perspective through which we view our experience. An example of a paradigm is one with which most of us are familiar. Prior to Galileo, the world was viewed through a paradigm that said that the sun travels around the earth. The relationship of celestial bodies to one another had an impact on other aspects of life and society in that period. In Galileo's time, the paradigm for governance placed the king at the center of the economy, law, and culture much as the earth was seen to be at the center of the universe. In addition, the father was considered the center of the family, and the Church was the center of morals, values, and lifestyle. This mono-centric view of the world was shattered when Galileo proposed a new paradigm which viewed the earth as only one of many entities circling the sun. If this way of viewing the universe were correct, then many centers could exist for interpreting the law, generating economic resources, managing the family, and choosing how to worship. The changing paradigm made available multiple sources of power and possibility.

Paradigms that have shifted in our lifetime have included the increased role of women in families, communities, and businesses; the view of Russia as an ally and partner; and the belief that all Americans are entitled to civil rights and voting privileges. Just as these changing conceptual frameworks have led to new thinking and behavior, so too, the paradigm regarding leadership will have to change in order to transform our economic and social conditions.

Before a shift in paradigm can take place, we have to see the old one, know it for what it is, and recognize its impact on our perceptions of the world. As the fish is the last species to know water, so we find it difficult to perceive the paradigms in which we function. Here are three tenets of an old paradigm of leadership. As we heighten our awareness of them we can begin to see how they shape our considerations about becoming a leader.

1. *Leaders Are Born and Not Made*

This is the silver-spoon theory of leadership. In the old paradigm, leaders must have had the correct lineage and been endowed from birth with the look, personality, and sensibility of power and authority.

2. *Good Management Makes Successful Organizations*

The nineteenth-century model of organization still pervades our institutions. In this paradigm, we assume that if we have efficient management, produce short-term results, and streamline our systems, we will be successful.

3. *Failure Is to Be Avoided at All Costs*

Most of us have been raised to believe that we must never fail. If we make mistakes they should be hidden, swept under the rug, denied, or passed on to others. In this paradigm, organizational behavior is characterized by risk avoidance and fear.

How many times have we viewed our experience through the lens of these ideas? We forget that they are not truths written in stone but merely ideas that can be challenged, replaced, or ignored. In this chapter, we have the opportunity to create a new paradigm of leadership, one that will validate our experience and support doing the right thing rather than doing things right, that will encourage taking risks and learning from failure.

In order to shift our thinking and behavior from one paradigm to another, we first need to become aware of the pervasiveness of our old way of thinking. Next we will define the new paradigm and finally take action based on the assumptions embedded in the new. In the following exercises, we shift to a new paradigm of leadership in which leaders are created through a process of transformation, in which leaders rather than managers are at the helm of new organizations, and in which failure is valued as a source of learning and growth.

Leaders Are Made by Learning How to Learn—An Exercise

We begin by exploring your capacity to learn something new. As adults we rarely have the opportunity to place ourselves in the role of learner. Some of us have gone back to school to earn a degree or participate in a special institute. We have attended in-service or on-the-job educational programs in our company or organization. But, too often, the learning environment we encounter is low-risk and protected. We frequently passively skate through without having to confront our basic assumptions.

We advocate a different quality of learning experience. As we see it, active, risky, self-conscious, and committed learning is required in order to become the leaders demanded by today's complex and crisis-oriented environment. The learning we mean is much more than the absorption of a body of knowledge or the mastery of a discipline. It is seeing the world simultaneously as it is and as it can be, understanding the distinction between the two, and acting to bridge the gap. It is the complete deployment of ourselves to realize the full promise of life.

Ideally, if you want to know how you learn, you might pursue an activity you believed you could never perform. For example, you might participate for the first time in an Outward Bound program, or learn skiing, white-water rafting, mountain climbing, or bungee jumping. These dramatic physical challenges will teach you all you need to know about your learning style and confront you with your assumptions about yourself, turning your world upside down. Learning to become a leader may take just that!

If you have the opportunity to choose a physically demanding learning challenge, go right ahead. We encourage you to take the risk. However, you need not leap giant buildings in a single bound in order to learn about yourself. Volunteer to give a speech, run a meeting, act in a local theater company, learn to type, spend time getting to know people you disagree with, drive to an unknown community, or spend a day alone in unfamiliar territory. If your life permits, test yourself with a mode of behavior that is very different from one you are used to. It will give you the insights you need to learn about your learning style.

Learning to Lead

As you take on a new and challenging experience, listen to your own voice. Observe your feelings, your reactions, and your inner dialogue. When it is over, spend time reflecting on what happened. What are your memories of the experience? Take time to think about what you did, what it felt like, and how you did it. If you cannot engage a new experience, remember when you learned something new and experienced a departure from your normal routine. Reflect either on your experience from the past or on one you tried out for this exercise.

Questions to Consider

A. Begin by describing in detail the challenge, the new experience, and the risk you took as the focus of this reflection.

....

....

....

....

....

....

....

....

....

....

B. What were your fears before you began the experience? How did those fears change and evolve throughout the experience?

....

....

....

....

....

....

....

....

....

....

C. What had others told you about yourself that either supported or undermined your confidence?

....

....

....

....

....

....

....

....

....

....

D. What seemed to be the greatest risk before you started? How did the risks change as you proceeded through the experience?

....

....

....

....

....

....

....

....

....

....

E. What people, circumstances, actions, and events most supported your learning? Which ones blocked your learning?

....

....

....

....

....

....

....

....

....

....

F. What was it about your thinking and behavior that most contributed to your learning? Which ones blocked your learning?

....

....

....

....

....

....

....

....

....

....

G. At what point did you know you were successful? How did you know you were successful?

....

....

....

....

....

....

....

....

....

H. What were the high points, the joys, and the payoffs for the risks you took?

....

....

....

....

....

....

....

....

....

I. How did your image of yourself change as a result of the experience?

....

....

....

....

....

....

....

....

....

....

J. What new experiences grew out of this one? How did you change because of what you learned?

....

....

....

....

....

....

....

....

....

....

....

....

Learning to become a leader is the same as risking a new challenge. Your answers to these questions can give you information about your approach to learning from new experiences. You can see the behaviors, the thinking, and the support it will take to enable you to overcome your fears. You can also see the rewards that are available from the chances you took.

Learning Modes—An Exercise

Each of us has our own way of learning something new. How many times have we argued with otherwise loving companions when they have told us how to go about a new project that we planned in a completely different way! Gib Akin, associate professor at the McIntire School of Commerce, University of Virginia, studied the learning experiences of sixty managers. Writing for *Organizational Dynamics*, Akin found that the manager's descriptions were "surprisingly congruous. . . . Learning is experienced as a personal transformation. A person does not gather learnings as possessions but rather becomes a new person. . . . To learn is not to have, it is to be." Here are the variety of ways that managers learn, according to Akin's research:

- **Emulation,** in which one emulates either someone one knows or a historical or public figure;
- **Role taking,** in which one has a conception of what one should do and does it;
- **Practical accomplishment,** in which one sees a problem as an opportunity and learns through the experience of dealing with it;
- **Validation,** in which one tests concepts by applying them and learns after the fact;
- **Anticipation,** in which one develops a concept and then applies it, learning before acting;
- **Personal growth,** in which one is less concerned with specific skills than with self-understanding and the "transformation of values and attitudes";
- **Scientific learning,** in which one observes, conceptualizes on the basis of one's observations, then experiments to gather new data, with a primary focus on truth.

Each of Akin's modes of learning is valid for different circumstances and different learning needs. Each mode has positive and negative qualities that determine when it is appropriate to use. In the following chart, identify a situation in which you have used each mode for yourself and reflect on the positive and negative aspects of each mode.

For example, it is said that Bill Clinton emulated John Kennedy to learn his leadership style. A positive aspect of this mode of learning for Clinton was that Kennedy's image as an agent of change was one worth emulating. However, Kennedy's personal life and association with many women outside his marriage is not a trait that Clinton can afford to emulate. Therefore emulation has its limits. If we use this mode, we need to carefully choose the characteristics we emulate.

Modes of Learning Chart

Mode	Situation	Positive Aspect	Negative Aspect
Emulation			
Role taking			
Practical Accomplishment			
Validation			
Anticipation			
Personal Growth			
Scientific Learning			

As you are learning to become a leader, review this chart and choose the way you would like to learn. Do you want to find a mentor to emulate? Is it best for you to jump in feet first and learn through practical accomplishment? Would you rather focus on self-understanding or on practical skills to transform yourself? Choose the mode or modes that best serve your style and circumstances.

A Learning Style Presentation—An Exercise

You have now reflected on learning something new and gained an understanding of what it will take for you to learn to be a leader. You have also reviewed different modes of learning to discover their appropriate uses for your circumstances. The following activity will enable you to consolidate your knowledge of how you approach learning. Introduce yourself to a friend, colleague, or small group by filling in the following narrative. If you are working alone, write the description of yourself as if you were presenting it to others. Try to communicate to others what you know about your learning style. Use this as an opportunity to receive feedback from the group or for self-reflection if you are working alone.

Learning Style Presentation

Hello, my name is .... I'd like to introduce myself and tell you about how I approach a risky learning situation. I'd also like to tell you about the learning modes that I find most useful for me. I'd like your feedback on my learning style based on your knowledge of me.

The last important learning experience I had was when ....

....

....

What I learned from that experience was ....

....

....

I enjoy learning new things when I feel ....

....

....

The modes I like to use to learn something new are ....

....

....

In order to feel safe enough to try something new and possibly threatening I need ....

....

....

I have the most difficulty learning something new when ....

....

....

Learning to Lead

I take the most pride and joy from learning when I have................................

....

....

The next time I am in a new learning situation I would like your support by.............

....

....

The next challenge I would like to face with your support is ....

....

....

The managers Akin interviewed cited two basic motivations for learning. The first was a need to know, which they described as "rather like a thirst or hunger gnawing at them, sometimes dominating their attention until satisfied." The second was a "sense of role," which stems from "a person's perception of the gap between what he or she is, and what he or she should be."

In other words, the managers knew that they were not fulfilling their own potential, not expressing themselves fully—and they knew that learning was the way out of the trap, requiring them to take a major step toward self-expression. They saw learning as something intimately connected with self. No one taught them that in school. They had to teach themselves. Somehow they had reached a point in life where they knew they had to learn new things—it was either that or admit they had settled for less than they were capable of. If you can accept all that, as these managers did, the next step is to assume responsibility for your education yourself.

Failure—The Springboard of Hope

Perhaps the most impressive and memorable quality of leaders is the way they respond to failure. Like Karl Wallenda, the great tightrope aerialist—whose life was at stake each time he walked the tightrope—leaders put all their energies into their task. As Wallenda put it in 1978 just before he fell to his death, "Being on the tightrope is living; everything else is waiting."

82

Leaders live their own version of the tightrope. They simply don't think about failure. One of them said during an interview that "a mistake is just another way of doing things." Another said, "If I have an art form of leadership, it is to make as many mistakes as quickly as I can in order to learn."

Shortly after Wallenda fell to his death in 1978 traversing a 75-foot highwire in downtown San Juan, Puerto Rico, his wife, also an aerialist, discussed that fateful San Juan walk, "perhaps his most dangerous." She recalled: "All Karl thought about for three straight months prior to it was *falling*. It was the first time he'd ever thought about that, and it seemed to me that he put all his energies into *not falling* rather than walking the tightrope." From what we know about successful leaders, it is clear that when Karl Wallenda poured his energies into *not falling* rather than walking the tightrope, he was virtually destined to fall.

An example of the "Wallenda factor" comes in an interview with Fletcher Byrom, who recently retired from the presidency of the Koppers Company, a diversified engineering, construction, and chemicals company. When asked about the "hardest decision he ever had to make," he responded this way:

> I don't know what a hard decision is. I may be a strange animal but I don't worry. Whenever I make a decision, I start out recognizing there's a strong likelihood I'm going to be wrong. All I can do is the best I can. To worry puts obstacles in the way of clear thinking.

Or consider Ray Meyer—perhaps the winningest coach in college basketball, who led De-Paul University to forty-two consecutive winning seasons. When his team dropped its first game after twenty-nine straight home court victories, his response was: "Great! Now we can start concentrating on winning, *not* on not losing." Meyer reframes for us the capacity to embrace positive goals, to pour one's energies into the task, not looking behind and dredging up excuses for past events.

For a lot of people, the word "failure" carries with it a finality, the absence of movement characteristic of a dead thing, to which the automatic human reaction is helpless discouragement. But for the successful leader, failure is a beginning, the springboard of hope.

John Cleese, in addition to his memorable comic turns in movies and with Monty Python, writes and produces organizational development programs that combine humor and wisdom. In a piece for *Forbes* magazine several years ago, he exhorted heads of organizations to adopt a policy of "No More Mistakes and You're Through." He points out that creativity, innovation, and human progress is based on learning from failure. The scientific method, creativity in the arts, and individual human growth includes error and adjustment based on learning. Cleese observes:

> It's self-evident that if we can't take the risk of saying or doing something wrong, our creativity goes right out the window. . . . The essence of creativity is not the possession of some special talent, it is much more the ability to play. . . . In organizations where mistakes are not allowed, you get two types of counterproductive behavior. First, since mistakes are "bad" if they're committed by the people at the top, people can pretend that no mistake has been made. So it doesn't get fixed. Second, if they're committed by people lower down in the organization, mistakes get concealed.

For an organization to truly encourage independent thinking that will produce the best decisions and the wisest policies, it must encourage learning and the mistakes it engenders.

Patterns of Failure—An Exercise

Where did our attitudes and beliefs about mistakes, failure, disappointments, and wrong turns begin? Observing a young child begin to walk is a lesson in failure. The infant falls hundreds of times before she gets the knack of standing on two feet and propelling forward or backward. She does not stop to feel wrong, guilty, or embarrassed. She is determined to walk. Each fall is only a necessary part of the learning process. Remember learning to ride a bicycle? It was the same story. We did not stop to analyze our failures. We did not refuse to ride again after every skinned knee. We continued to weave and wobble and get back on the bike again until we mastered the bicycle and, at the same time, ourselves.

As we have grown into adulthood, we have learned a very different attitude toward mistakes. Our adult view of failure blocks our ability to take risks, to stand up for what we know is true, and respond to situations that demand leadership. Where did we learn this view of failure? How have our patterns been reinforced throughout our adult life?

The following exercise should be carried out with a spouse, partner, or in small groups of colleagues. The purpose is to help you discover the origins of your patterns regarding failure. First, read the instructions to yourself. In this guided imagery, please accept the insights you gain, the images you see, and the feelings you experience as being right and appropriate for you. *There are no mistakes.* You may fall asleep, or you may not see any pictures or feel any sensations. You may only see a color or hear a sound, or you may have some insight into your patterns regarding failure. Whatever happens is fine. Just follow the instructions as they are read by your partner or group leader and accept whatever comes from the experience.

If you are working on this activity in a group, one person should volunteer to read the instructions aloud to the group as everyone else goes through the process. If you are with a partner, one person should read the instructions while the other person follows the internal journey. Next, the partner will have an opportunity to go through the process.

In the course of this guided imagery, you or others may experience strong feelings. Do not open your eyes or interrupt the exercise. Just let the feelings be part of the process and continue with it.

Guided Imagery Instructions

Sit in a comfortable position in a chair with your back against the chair and your feet firmly on the floor. (Pause). Good.

Uncross your legs and hands and rest them in a relaxed position on your lap.

Gently let your eyes close. Take several deep breaths and slowly release them. (Pause). With each breath let your eyes relax and let your body release all the tension that is there. (Pause). Good.

Notice any sounds and movement in the room and let your attention go.

Let any thoughts you have come into your consciousness and release them. (Pause). Good.

Let any emotions you have come into your consciousness and release them. (Pause). Thank you.

Let any pictures from the past come into your consciousness and release them. (Pause). Good.

Now you are sitting comfortably in your chair. You have let go of any noises and movement in the room. You have released all tension and inner signals.

Now focus your attention on your feet and legs. If there is any tension there, release it. (Pause). Good.

Now focus your attention on your abdomen and lower body. If there is any tension there, release it.

Now focus your attention on your chest, shoulders, and arms. If there is any tension there, release it. (Pause). Good.

Now focus your attention on your neck, head, and face. If there is any tension there, release it.

Now you are fully relaxed and open to whatever is there for you. (Pause). Good.

Remember a time when you failed at something. Just let the memory come into your consciousness. Stay with the memory for a minute or two. (Pause). Notice who is there with you. (Pause). Notice how you felt.

Remember another time when you failed at something. (Pause). Just let the memory come into your consciousness. Stay with the memory for a minute or two. (Pause). Notice who is there with you. (Pause). Notice how you felt. (Pause). Good.

Remember a time when you were a failure. Just let the memory come into your consciousness. Stay with the memory for a minute or two. (Pause). Notice who told you that you were a failure. (Pause). Notice how you felt.

Let any feelings you have associated with these incidents come up and release them. (Pause). Good.

If you have anything to say to the person who told you that you were a failure, say it to them in your mind now. (Pause). Good.

Remember a time when someone you were close to was a failure. Just let the memory come into your consciousness. (Pause). Who told them they were a failure? Stay with the memory for a minute or two. Notice what it was they thought was a failure. (Pause). Notice how they felt. (Pause). Notice how you felt.

If you have any feelings about failure that you want to say goodbye to, say goodbye now. (Pause). Good.

Let go of all the images you have had in your mind and relax. (Pause). Good.

Remain in a relaxed, peaceful position now. (Pause). Just let any feelings, thoughts, or pictures come to the surface and release them.

Now begin to feel the back of the chair next to your body and the floor under your feet. (Pause). Good.

Begin to return your attention to the room.

Begin to hear the noises in the room. Notice the movement. (Pause). Good.

As I count to five, return your attention to the room. One. (Pause). Two. (Pause). Three. (Pause). Four. (Pause). Five. Open your eyes, and say hello to someone here in the room.

Turn to someone next to you and share what each of you learned from this exercise. You may have had a number of insights, images, and feelings come to the surface in this exercise. It is now time to take a look at the origins of your views on failure and how they affect your current life.

Labeling an action or person a "failure" is an arbitrary decision that you or someone else made sometime in the past. You or others then attached meanings, associations, decisions, and feelings to the concept of failure. In the present, you can transform your past associations, ideas, and decisions about failure to ones that are more useful to becoming a leader. Rather than getting stuck, feeling depressed, denigrating yourself, or using the event as evidence of your low self-worth, consider an alternative: Failure is an opportunity to learn, to change course, and to discover new options for yourself.

Each of us makes many mistakes in the course of each day. Some we notice because we are sensitive to a particular mistake or because someone has called attention to it. However, in shifting our paradigm about leadership we have an opportunity to change our view of failure. We have a choice: We can consider each mistake a natural part of life from which we can learn and grow, or we can use failure as evidence of our lack of self-worth.

David Hare, the playwright, told a wonderful story about Joe Papp, impresario and director of the New York Shakespeare Festival, at a memorial for Papp just after his death in November 1991:

> The greatest thing Joe ever did was when we did "The Knife." There was a party afterward and the reviews were read. The *Times* review was absolutely dismal. He read it out line by line and the whole room went completely silent. It meant that we had lost over a million dollars. At the end he said, "That is not what I call a good review." Then he turned to me and said, "What do you want to do in my theater next?"

In shifting to a new paradigm of failure, discuss with your partner or small group the insights that you gained from your greatest failure.

In Chapter Three we investigated the models and patterns of leadership we learned in our families. Now we need to probe our family experiences regarding failure. First you may want to reflect on the questions below on your own, thinking through the answers for yourself. Next you may want to discuss your answers with family members and friends. Consider their insights into your history. Compare your memories with the remembrances of others.

Questions to Consider

A. What were the messages about failure in your family? What messages were sent to you? What messages were sent to others?

....

....

....

....

....

....

....

....

B. How were you treated when you failed?

....

....

....

....

....

....

....

....

C. What decisions did you make about failure that were related to you or to others?

....

....

....

....

. . . .

. . . .

. . . .

. . . .

D. How have you perpetuated these early family views of failure in your own personal life or relationships?

. . . .

. . . .

. . . .

. . . .

. . . .

. . . .

. . . .

In your professional life?

. . . .

. . . .

. . . .

. . . .

. . . .

. . . .

In the lives of your children?

. . . .

. . . .

....

....

....

....

....

....

In the lives of your colleagues and subordinates?

....

....

....

....

....

....

....

E. Who told you that you were a failure or that you should never fail?

....

....

....

....

....

....

....

F. What was it about that person's own life that motivated him or her to teach you about failure?

....

....

....

....

....

....

....

....

G. How were they serving their needs in telling you about failure?

....

....

....

....

....

....

....

....

H. What did you do with the information they gave you about failure?

....

....

....

....

....

· ·

· ·

· ·

It may be difficult to answer these questions about the past and about family members who loved you and whom you loved. But it is important to trace the roots of your belief system so that you can see yourself realistically and transform your way of thinking about yourself.

As you reveal your thinking and feeling about failure, you will begin to see an alternative to your old paradigm. It takes a conscious effort to think about mistakes, problems, and failure in a new way. The next exercise may help you make this paradigmatic shift.

Leadership Checklist—An Exercise

John Sculley, former CEO of Apple Computer, discusses his approach to fostering higher states of creativity within an organization. He describes how he deals with problems in an interview in *Fortune* magazine in September 1987:

> Defensiveness is the bane of all passion-filled creative work. We (at Apple) keep defenses down in several ways. One way is by thinking about problems differently—not as negatives, for example. We are thinking of giving people medals for problem finding, not just problem solving. Our world moves so fast that new problems are being created all the time. The people who find them have tremendous powers of creative observation.

Take a look at your organization's paradigm for leadership by examining how it fosters creativity. Since mistakes are an outcome of risk taking and creativity, we must also look at attitudes toward failure. We have created a checklist for you to use in assessing the creativity of your organization. Before completing the creativity checklist, we suggest you conduct an audit of the ways failure and mistakes are viewed in your organization. Conduct the audit for one week. Note every failure, problem, or mistake that you encounter; whether you are responsible or someone else is "to blame"; and whether or not the problem is seen as an opportunity for a creative solution. Questions for the audit are as follows:

A. Describe the failure or problem:

· ·

· ·

....

....

B. Indicate the points of view, attitudes, positions, and reactions by leadership to the failure or problem:

....

....

....

....

C. Indicate how you see the problem, how you feel about it, your reaction to it:

....

....

....

....

D. Describe an alternative point of view. Look for ways to see the failure as an opportunity, create a learning perspective, or put a positive cast to the incident, no matter how dire the situation:

....

....

....

....

You may involve others in this audit, but all your responses should be your own. When you have completed the audit, share your results with colleagues who may also have conducted one. Ask for feedback from others and compare your perceptions with them. Complete the checklist below and use it as a reminder of alternative points of view about creativity when you encounter the next problem.

In the following exercise you can practice transforming your attitude about failure. Changing this attitude is one of the prerequisites to shifting your leadership paradigm. The process for living in a new paradigm includes recognizing the old paradigm, giving up old ways of thinking, creating alternative points of view, and adopting new behaviors.

The Creativity Checklist

Problem Description	Organizational Attitude	Your Attitude	Opportunity For Creativity
1.			
....	....	....	....
....	....	....	....
....	....	....	....
....	....	....	....
2.			
....	....	....	....
....	....	....	....
....	....	....	....
3.			
....	....	....	....
....	....	....	....
....	....	....	....
4.			
....	....	....	....
....	....	....	....
....	....	....	....
5.			
....	....	....	....
....	....	....	....
6.			
....	....	....	....
....	....	....	....

You can also stimulate changes in your organization. Encourage your colleagues to revise their thinking about mistakes. Point out the creative solutions that can be found by learning from mistakes and using knowledge to generate alternatives.

Arnold Hiatt, chairman of Stride Rite Corporation—the 50-year-old successful U.S. footwear company—puts it this way in an interview:

> My personal struggle has always been how far to let someone else go. I'll see someone in the company doing something I know isn't right, because I've been there myself too many times before. But then I grit my teeth and remind myself that I never learned anything by listening to someone else preach. The mistakes I made were my best teacher by far.
>
> (Arnold Hiatt, *Harvard Business Review,* March–April 1992)

Learning, creativity, involvement, innovation, flexibility, and communication are all by-products of an openness to mistakes, problems and failures. The successful leaders of our times know that there are no more scripts to follow, no cut-and-dried solutions to adopt. It is up to all of us to create the answers by working together and using our own resources. The answers to the AIDS crisis, ethnic cleansing in Yugoslavia, the starvation in poor nations, the gang warfare in our cities, and the homelessness of our urban populations will come from the lessons we learn from our failures.

The Lifeline—An Exercise

Knowing ourselves requires a knowledge of our history and an acknowledgment of our past. Our talents for leadership and our ability to take on a leadership role were developed over time and began early in our lives. We did not spring full grown as leaders from Zeus's temple. In a previous exercise in this chapter, we explored our family history and the models of leadership we learned from our parents and other family members. In Chapter Three we explored our family trees in detail. Now it is time to look into your personal experience and create a lifeline that will reveal the factors that shaped your view of yourself as a leader and point to the strengths you bring from those early experiences.

Our friend and colleague Will Schultz has developed an exercise for his book, *The Human Element,* that will deepen your awareness of the lessons you learned from your past and how they translate into your role as a leader.

Learning to Lead

- Think about or draw a picture of yourself as far back as you can remember. Shut your eyes and picture yourself at the very earliest age.

....
....
....
....

- In your beginning group, your family: What was your birth order? What was your role in the family, when your parents were home? When they were not home? When no one else was home?

....
....
....
....

- With your playmates: Were you a leader? Dominant? Shy? Well liked? Ignored? Rejected? Admired? Good at sports? Good at school? A rebel?

....
....
....
....

- Was your size a factor? Your appearance? Your abilities or lack of abilities? Your gender? Your ethnic group? Did you have a nickname?

....
....
....
....

- Was there a change when the other sex was present? When dating began? Were you popular? Unwanted? A loner? Party goer? Sought out? Ignored? (*Reflect on how much of your present behavior regarding leadership is more understandable in light of these early events.*)

....

....

....

....

- Follow this series of questions for all your social groups throughout your life, first with people older than you, then with peers, then with people younger than you, or those with lower status or position.

....

....

....

....

- When you complete this image, stand back and observe the evolutionary lines. What role have you typically played? Which are you good at? Which are you poor at? Which do you enjoy? Which do you avoid?

....

....

....

....

- How do people typically treat you? In what ways do all people treat you the same? In what ways do certain types of people treat you the same?

....

....

....

....

- How do you anticipate people will respond to you? What types of reactions do you typically elicit—fatherly, sexual, sisterly, competitive, sympathetic, motherly, helper, victim, nasty, critical?

....

....

....

. . . .

Questions to Consider

A. Given these memories, describe the type of leader you could be that would make maximum use of your strengths and roles:

. . . .

. . . .

. . . .

. . . .

B. What are the ways you would, initially at least, want others to respond to you?

. . . .

. . . .

. . . .

. . . .

C. What are the experiences from the past you would want to overcome to be a more effective leader?

. . . .

. . . .

. . . .

. . . .

The process of knowing ourselves continues as we grow into leadership roles. New memories emerge from the recesses of our minds, new insights about our past may also occur. As they do, you may want to record them for a time of reflection.

In the next chapter, we will discover the power of vision in enabling leaders to realize their intentions. Solutions to seemingly impossible problems grow from dreams that leaders have of how it could be. Leaders are the initiators and communicators of visions for change.

Chapter 5

Creating and Communicating a Vision

In which we discover the power of a vision, create our own vision for our organization, and place ourselves inside that vision to dream a dream for our own lives.

All men dream; but not equally.
Those who dream by night in the dusty recesses
   of their minds
Awake to find that it was vanity;
But the dreamers of day are dangerous men,
That they may act their dreams with open
   eyes to make it possible.

T. E. Lawrence

A Passionate Commitment to Vision

Warren Bennis has spent the last thirteen years talking with leaders, including Jim Burke at Johnson & Johnson, John Sculley when he was at Apple, television producer Norman Lear, and over a hundred other men and women, some famous and some not. In the course of his research, something emerged about the current crop of leaders, and about the kind of leadership that will be necessary to forge the future. While leaders come in every size, shape, and disposition—short, tall, neat, sloppy, young, old, male, and female—there is at least one ingredient that every leader shared: concern with a guiding purpose, an overarching vision. They were more than goal directed, they were vision directed.

Learning to Lead

Leaders are the most results-oriented individuals in the world, and results get attention. Their visions or intentions are compelling and pull people toward them. Intensity coupled with commitment is magnetic. These intense personalities do not have to coerce people to pay attention; they are so intent on what they are doing that, like a child completely absorbed with creating a sand castle in a sandbox, they draw others in.

We think of it this way: *Leaders manage the dream.* All leaders have the capacity to create a compelling vision, one that takes people to a new place, then translates that vision into reality. Peter Drucker said that the first task of a leader is to define the mission. Max DePree, CEO of Herman Miller, wrote in *Leadership Is an Art,* "The first responsibility of a leader is to define reality. The last is to say thank you. In between, the leader is a servant."

Vision *grabs.* Initially it grabs the leader, and the ability to communicate it ultimately enables others also to get on the bandwagon. Warren Bennis visited Ray Kroc at "Hamburger U" in Elk Grove, Illinois, near Chicago, where McDonald's employees can get a "Bachelor of hamburgerology with a minor in french fries." Kroc spoke of his initial vision. He was already a tremendously successful paper-cup manufacturer when he began manufacturing milkshake machines. He met the McDonald brothers, who owned a chain of milkshake parlors, and that collision of cups and shakes set off the spark—a phenomenon we now know as McDonald's. When asked what leads to such serendipitous notions, Kroc answered:

> I can't pretend to know what it is. Certainly it is not some divine vision. Perhaps it's a combination of your background, your instincts and your dreams. Whatever it was at that moment, I suppose I became an entrepreneur and decided to go for broke.

Another of Warren Bennis's interviewees was Sergio Comissioná, the renowned conductor, when he was with the Houston Symphony Orchestra. For a long time he refused to be interviewed, which was remarkable in and of itself. He would not respond to letters; he would not respond to phone calls. After many months Warren was able to get in touch with two of his musicians. When asked what Comissioná was like, they answered, "Terrific." But when asked why, they wavered. Finally they said, "Because he does not waste our time."

That simple declarative sentence at first seemed insignificant. But when we finally watched him conduct and teach his master classes, we began to understand the full meaning of that phrase "he does not waste our time." It became clear that Comissioná transmits an unbri-

100

dled clarity about what he wants from the players. He knows precisely and emphatically what he wants to hear at any given time. This fixation with and undeviating attention to outcome—some would call it an obsession—is only possible if one knows what one wants. That can come only from vision or, as one member of Comissioná's orchestra referred to it, from "the maestro's tapestry of intentions." This passion of leaders recalls a character from Shaw's *Man and Superman:*

> This is the true joy in life, the being used for a purpose recognized by yourself as a mighty one; the being a force of nature instead of a feverish selfish little clod of ailments and grievances complaining that the world will not devote itself to making you happy. I want to be thoroughly used up when I die, for the harder I work the more I live. I rejoice in life for its own sake. Life is no "brief candle" to me. It is a sort of splendid torch which I have got hold of for the moment, and I want to make it burn as brightly as possible before handing it on to future generations.
> (George Bernard Shaw, *Man and Superman*)

There is a high, intense filament we notice in our leaders—similar to Comissioná's passion about the "right" tone. Sometimes it burns only within the range of their vision, and outside that range they can be as dull or interesting as anyone else. A basic ingredient of leadership is *passion*—the underlying passion for the promises of life, combined with a very particular passion for a vocation, a profession, a course of action. The leader loves what he or she does and loves doing it. Tolstoy said that hopes are the dreams of the waking man. Without hope, we cannot survive, much less progress. The leader who communicates passion gives hope and inspiration to other people. Passion can be lived through enthusiasm, through vitality, through demonstrated and unswerving commitment to a vision.

Visions seem to bring about confidence on the part of employees, confidence that instills in them a belief that they are capable of performing to their full potential. Edwin H. Land, founder of Polaroid, said: "The first thing you naturally do is teach the person to feel that the undertaking is manifestly important and nearly impossible. . . . That draws out the kind of drives that make people strong, that put you in pursuit intellectually."

Vision animates, inspirits, and transforms purpose into action. Lincoln Kirstein, founder of the New York City Ballet and School, said: "My whole life has been trying to learn how things are done. What I love about ballet is not that it looks pretty. It's the method in it. Ballet is about how to behave." One of his associates said about him: "He has a power of concentration the likes of which I've never seen. He always knew what he wanted." That is why it was also said about Kirstein that he never "wastes your time."

Alignment of Others to Your Vision

"If you can dream it, you can do it." Walt Disney

This quote from Walt Disney figures high on a sign at the Epcot Center in Orlando, Florida. While it beckons the Don Quixote in us all, the idea is complete. Believing in one's dreams is not enough. There are a lot of intoxicating visions and noble intentions. Many people have rich and deeply textured agendas, but without communication nothing can be realized. Success requires the capacity to communicate a compelling image of a desired state of affairs—the kind of image that induces enthusiasm and commitment in others.

Leadership is a transaction between leaders and followers. Neither could exist without the other. We discovered that leaders *pay* attention as well as catch it. Even though they are commanding figures, the interaction between leader and led is far more complicated than the simple command: they each bring out the best in the other. The new style of leadership is not arbitrary or unilateral, but rather an impressive and subtle sweeping back and forth of energy, whether between maestro and musicians or CEO and staff. The transaction creates unity. Conductor and orchestra are one. Coach and team, leader and organization are one. That unified focus flows from the communication of a vision.

How do you capture the imagination of others? How do you communicate visions? How do you get people aligned behind an organization's overarching goals? How do you get an audience to recognize and accept an idea? The mastery of communication and empathy is inseparable from effective leadership.

Former CBS executive Barbara Corday leads through empathy, which she sees as particularly female:

> I think women generally see power in a different way than men. I don't have any need for personal power, especially over people. I want to have the kind of power that is my company working well, my staff working well. . . . As moms and wives and daughters we've been caretakers, and a lot of the caretakers in our lives were women, and we continue in caretaking roles even as we get successful in business. And that feels natural to us. I have always been very pleased and happy and proud of the fact that I not only know all the people who work for me, but I know their husbands'

and wives' names, and I know their children's names, and I know who's been sick, and I know what to ask. That's what's special to me in a work atmosphere. I think that's what people appreciate, and that's why they want to be there, and that's why they're loyal, and that's why they care about what they're doing. And I think that is peculiarly female.

Empathy isn't only the province of women. Former Lucky Stores CEO Don Ritchey said, "I think one of the biggest turn-ons for people is to know that their peers and particularly their bosses not only know they're there but know pretty intimately what they're doing and are involved with them on almost a daily basis, that it's a partnership, that you're really trying to run this thing well together, that if something goes wrong our goal is to fix it, not see who we can nail."

Communicating with meaning is the partner to empathic leadership in realizing a vision. Many leaders find a metaphor that embodies and implements their vision. For Darwin, the metaphor was a branching tree of evolution on which he could trace the rise of various species. William James viewed mental processes as a stream or river. John Locke focused on the falconer, whose release of a bird symbolized his "own emerging view of the creative process"—that is, the quest for human knowledge.

When Frank Dale took over the *Los Angeles Herald-Examiner,* Los Angeles' afternoon newspaper, a few years ago, they were just ending a bloody ten-year-old strike. Dale, the new president and publisher, had to go in through the back to greet his irksome staff. Listen to Dale's words in an interview with Warren Bennis:

A: I started the pattern the very first hour I was there. A new manager. . . . It so happened that the front door of the building was barricaded. It had not been open in eight years. I had to walk through the back door, have my fingerprints taken, my picture taken: "Welcome aboard, boss!" I went to the newsroom within the first hour and asked the people who were working to come and gather around me so I could introduce myself—I had no one else . . .

Q: You mean, you couldn't walk through the front door?

A: That's right. The lobby had been barricaded for over eight years. There was tremendous strife, people were killed, employees were killed and indeed, it was eventually some employees who had never been unionized or related to any union who simply said to each other over a beer one night: "We gotta quit shooting each other." And so, on a peace platform, they got the employees to vote for a settlement and eventually got the right to bargain and that was done. I called the people on duty at the time around the desk in an informal setting—I had no one to introduce me. . . . I did it myself so that I would be right there and without any forethought at all I said, "Maybe the first thing we ought to do is open up the front door." Everybody stood up and cheered. Grown men and women cried. That was a symbol, you see, that barricade was a symbol of defeat, of siege. And "let the sun in" was what I was saying. . . . And then I attempted to introduce myself again, thanked them for preserving the opportunity that I had been asked to take advantage of. Which is really what they did— when I let the sunshine in. . . .

A number of lessons can be drawn from the experiences of leaders. First, that *all* organizations depend on the existence of shared meanings and interpretations of reality, which facilitate coordinated action. The actions and symbols of leadership frame and mobilize meaning. Leaders articulate and define what has previously remained implicit or unsaid; then they invent images, metaphors, and models that provide a focus for new attention. By so doing, they consolidate or challenge prevailing wisdom. In short, an *essential* factor in leadership is the ability to influence and *organize meaning* for the members of the organization.

What we mean by "meaning" goes far beyond what is usually meant by "communication." For one thing, it has little to do with "facts" or even "knowing." Facts and knowing have to do with technique, with methodology, with "knowing how to do things." That is useful, even necessary, and undeniably occupies an important place in today's scheme of things. But thinking is emphatically closer to meaning than knowing is. Thinking prepares one for what is to be done, for what ought to be done. Thinking, though it may be unsettling and dangerous to the established order, is constructive: it challenges old conventions by suggesting new directions, new visions. To depend on facts without thinking may seem safe and secure, but in the long run it is dangerously unconstructive because it has nothing to say about *direction*. The distinctive role of leadership, especially in a volatile environment, is to focus on "know-why" before "know-how." This distinction illustrates, once again, one of the key differences between leaders and managers.

What we see and experience in today's organizational landscape are cumbersome bureaucracies that more often than not demonstrate the mismanagement of meaning. A "great idea" is hatched. Responsibility is delegated. Then it is delegated again. Then it is redelegated.

By the time the great idea is carried out it is certainly not what the leaders intended or anticipated. This "Pinocchio effect" is the bane of many creators who, like Gepetto the puppet maker, are confronted with distended, distorted versions of their original plans. Lack of clarity makes bureaucracies little more than mechanisms for the evasion of responsibility and guilt.

Communication creates meaning for people. Or it should. It is the only way any group, small or large, can become aligned behind the overarching goals of an organization. Getting the message across unequivocally at every level is an absolute key. Basically it is what the creative process is all about.

Your Organizational Vision—An Exercise

Leaders are the kind of people to whom others are drawn—not because of their personalities, but because they have a vision, a dream, a set of intentions, an agenda, a frame of reference. Clearly, when we are with these individuals, we sense an extraordinary focus of commitment, which attracts us to them. It is often said of these leaders that they make us want to join with them: They enroll us in their vision.

By vision we mean a picture that can be seen with the mind's eye. We use vision rather than "mission" or "goals" because a vision can be *pictured*—it has substance, form, and color. The visual literacy experts tell us that the source of over 85 percent of the information we absorb is visual. Our eyes are the ports to our minds. Leaders understand the power of the visual and use it to attract others to their dream.

John Sculley, former chairman of Apple Computer Company, drew his vision into Apple's planning process. He describes one of six management principles he employed to lead Apple into an extraordinary future, as follows:

> *Don't give people goals:* tell them which way to go. We want people to reach ideas they haven't dreamed of yet. Unlike most corporations, we don't so much try to define our identity: we try to make it recognizable—not too concrete. So we talk endlessly—and aphoristically—about what we do: "We build people, not computers" or "The best way to predict the future is to invent it." Most corporate planners decide where the company should go in the next year or two by peering into the company's past and making judgments and extrapolations based on their experiences. We ask ourselves, What will the next five years be like? We create in our minds a portrait of

the economy, our industry, and our company. Then we move back into
the present envisioning what we have to do to get to the future.

A vision is a portrait of the future to which you can commit. It is the articulation of your values. It empowers you and inspires you to do your job and contribute ideas or actions beyond yourself. In this exercise you will have an opportunity to create a vision for your organizations and your job.

We would like you to begin with an encompassing vision for your organization. To complete this exercise you must go beyond your part in the play. From where you sit, you may see only a small piece of the action. Expand your view to include the entire organization— all the people, all the functions, all the results that are possible. In creating a vision statement for your organization, consider the following criteria:

- A vision engages your heart and your spirit.
- A vision taps into embedded concerns and needs.
- A vision asserts what you and your colleagues want to create.
- A vision is something worth going for.
- A vision provides meaning to the work you and your colleagues do.
- By definition a vision is a little cloudy and grand (if it were clear, it wouldn't be a vision).
- A vision is simple.
- A vision is a living document that can always be expanded.
- A vision provides a starting place from which to get to more and more levels of specificity.
- A vision is based in two deep human needs: quality and dedication.

Your vision will be uniquely your own. In creating it, take a risk: be daring and reach for what you truly want for your organization and your own role in it. Your vision should speak to the needs of others in the organization, to the strivings and hopes that may be unexpressed but held within. If it touches their longings, if it resonates with what is deeply felt, it will have the power of a vision.

To create your vision answer the following questions. They will enable you to begin to form the images that will give power to your dream.

Questions to Consider

A. What is unique about your organization?

....

....

....

....

B. What are your values and how do they shape your priorities for the future?

....

....

....

....

....

....

....

C. What do your customers, your clients, or the people you serve really need that you could provide?

....

....

....

....

....

....

....

    D. What would make you personally commit your mind and heart to this vision over the next five to ten years?

....

....

....

....

    E. What do you really want your organization to accomplish so that you will be committed, aligned, and proud of your association with it?

....

....

....

....

....

....

....

....

In answering these questions, you will begin to describe your dream for the organization. Eventually you will edit your vision statement to be brief and simple. Ultimately it will be a few sentences, no more than a paragraph. You will need to focus on language that is vivid, clear, and communicative. However, to begin, just let the images flow. Do not censor yourself. Allow the poet and the dreamer in you to emerge.

Now that you have answers to these questions, you will be ready to shape your vision. There are several steps that will support you in creating your vision. Begin with your dream for the entire organization. Think big—picture the whole institution. Later, you will create a vision for your own job that is aligned with the larger vision.

1. To begin, find a place to work that is comfortable. Perhaps you have a special place at home or at the office where you like to think and where you have privacy. Some people like to envision in a quiet, natural setting. Others work best over a

cup of cappuccino at a favorite coffee house. You can select the spot that will be most conducive to leaving the present behind and projecting yourself into the future.

2. Begin by clearing your mind of present-day obstacles and difficulties. As soon as your mind begins to create a dream of the future, the part of your brain that is grounded in reality kicks in and tells you that you are being unrealistic, foolish, and embarrassing. Ask this reality-checking function to quiet itself for now, allowing you to go as far as you can with your hopes and wishes.

3. Picture the future five or ten years ahead. What is the world like? How does your organization fit in the changing environment? What can it contribute? How is it viewed by others? How does it feel to live inside the organization? What does it look like physically? How many people work there? What products and services do you deliver? What do you wish for your organization at this time in the future? You may want to close your eyes to get a deeper image of your vision. You may want to start writing and see what emerges. It may be more useful to talk to someone else as you create your view of the future.

Each of us has our own way of being creative. Some of us do not know what we think until we say it. Others need time to write, and in the writing learn how we envision the future. The artists among us may feel more comfortable drawing a sketch of the future. Some of us may want to just close our eyes and dream.

4. As your vision begins to unfold, capture it on paper or on a tape recorder. You may prefer to draw it on large flip-chart paper. You may write it as a narrative in the space provided on page 110. You may speak it to a friend and have your friend take notes. As it begins to emerge, develop it, embroider it, let it expand and fill out until it is complete. Do not edit or censor your vision. Just let it flow until you have created the images that are right for you.

5. Now go back and review the questions above and make sure you have fully developed all aspects of your vision that make it complete.

The vision you have just created is a living document. It is meant to be shared with others, tested in conversation, and presented to colleagues for their reactions. Find an opportunity to present your vision to those you wish to inspire. If you are working in a small group,

Learning to Lead

Your Vision for Your Organization

....
....
....
....
....
....
....
....
....
....
....
....
....
....
....
....
....
....
....
....
....
....

have each person share their vision. Look for commonalities. Identify major differences. Try to create a shared vision for the group with which each person can identify.

If you are working as a team, you will find it valuable to have a team vision. Use this process to create one by working together to answer these questions.

Try writing your vision then drawing it symbolically. Does it change when it is translated into nonverbal symbols? If so, how does it change and what are the nuances?

As a small group or team, you may want to communicate your vision to others in the organization. Your purpose is *not* to give them the "right" vision but to inspire them to envision the future for themselves. As a leader you may want to involve them in your vision. Ask them what they think of it. How would they change it? Does it excite and inspire them? You can be a model for them in creating their own vision, or allow them to find their place in yours.

You in Your Vision—An Exercise

Now that you have created a vision for your organization, it is time to place yourself in the image. Seeing yourself in ways that others may not see you is part of creating your personal vision. Dare to envision yourself where and how you truly want to be. Leadership is not only having a dream for others but claiming that dream and the role you want to play in it. Arlene Blum, leader of a woman's expedition to climb the Himalayas, has written beautifully about the power of a vision. At 3:29 P.M. on October 15, 1978, a team of ten women became the first American climbing team to reach the summit of Annapurna I, the tenth highest mountain in the world. Arlene Blum was the leader of the expedition. She and her partners created a vision for themselves that challenged the expectations of women. They not only believed that women could climb the Himalayas but placed themselves inside that vision and made it happen.

> As women, we faced a challenge even greater than the mountain. We had
> to believe in ourselves enough to make the attempt in spite of social con-
> vention and two hundred years of climbing history in which women were
> usually relegated to the sidelines.

Blum talks about how women had been told for years that they were not strong enough to carry heavy loads, that they didn't have the leadership experience and emotional stability necessary to climb the highest mountains.

> Our expedition would give ten women the chance to attempt one of the world's highest and most challenging peaks, as well as the experience necessary to plan future Himalayan climbs. If we succeeded, we would be the first Americans to climb Annapurna and the first American women to reach eight thousand meters (26,200 feet).

Arlene Blum and her team challenged two hundred years of assumptions about what was possible to create a vision for themselves that they ultimately achieved. We invite you to be daring in your vision for yourself.

The following exercise will support you in getting to the heart of your dreams. It has been adapted from the work Beth Jandernoa and Alain Gauthier have developed in their leadership courses, in which they enable participants to create a vision of their personal future.

You will remember the relaxation exercise from Chapter Four. We will use it now to enable you to gain access to your inner self. If you are working with a partner, ask your colleague to read the relaxation instructions to you so you can clear your mind of extraneous thoughts and feelings. Then you can repeat the process for your partner. If you are working alone, read the instructions below, then close your eyes and repeat the process as you remember it. You need not worry about getting all the instructions correct. The purpose of the exercise is for you to relax and let go of everything that may be obstructing your vision.

> Sit in a comfortable position in your chair with your back against the chair and your feet firmly on the floor. (Pause). Good.
>
> Uncross your legs and your hands and rest them in a relaxed position on your lap.
>
> Gently let your eyes close. Take several deep breaths and slowly release them. (Pause). With each breath let your eyes relax and let your body release all the tension that is there. (Pause). Good.
>
> Notice any sounds and movements in the room and let your attention go.
>
> Let any thoughts you have come into your consciousness and release them. (Pause). Good.
>
> Let any emotions you have come into your consciousness and release them.
>
> Let any pictures from the past come into your consciousness and release them. (Pause). Good.

Now you are sitting comfortably in your chair. You have let go of any noises and movement in the room. You have released all tension and inner signals.

Now focus your attention on your feet and legs. If there is any tension there, release it. (Pause). Good.

Now focus your attention on your abdomen and lower body. If there is any tension there, release it.

Now focus your attention on your chest, shoulders, and arms. If there is any tension there, release it. (Pause). Good.

Now focus your attention on your neck, head, and face. If there is any tension there, release it.

Remain in a relaxed, peaceful position now. Just let any feelings, thoughts, or pictures come to the surface and release them. (Pause). Good.

Now begin to feel the back of the chair next to your body and the floor under your feet.

Begin to return your attention to the room. (Pause). Good.

Hear the noises in the room. Notice the movement.

Count to five and return your attention to the room, open your eyes, look around. One. (Pause). Two. (Pause). Three. (Pause). Four. (Pause). Five. (Pause). Let yourself be here in the present, relaxed and open to your vision.

Now that you are relaxed and comfortable you can begin to create your vision. Remember that you should use a form of expression that is comfortable for you. Thinking and imagining to yourself, talking with a partner, writing or recording a narrative, and drawing or sculpting are all possible forms. The following questions can guide you in the creation of a personal vision. Some may not apply to you. We may not have included others that may be relevant to your life. Use these questions as a starting point for your envisioning process. It may be helpful to close your eyes after reading each section to let the answers come to you.

Self

Begin by imagining yourself living to your full potential, demonstrating all your talents, enjoying your strengths, being in your prime and your peak. What are the qualities you possess? How do you feel about yourself? What are you doing? How are you living? What brings you joy and happiness?

Relationship

Think of your closest relationship. Imagine a conversation that would best symbolize this relationship at its highest level. What do you hear, see, feel? Focus on the qualities you bring to this relationship. What do you offer the other person? What are the two of you doing? How are you contributing to each other? Extend this image to other important relationships.

Family

Bring your family into your vision. How do they seem to you? What are they doing? How has your relationship with them evolved? Notice their health and well being. What is most satisfying to you about your relationship with them? How are you contributing to each other? What is your greatest source of joy in your relationship with them?

Work Life

Focus now on your work life. Take a long-term perspective and consider the vision you have already created for your organization. How have you expressed what really matters to you in your work? What is the quality of your day-to-day life? How have you demonstrated your values? What have you achieved? What gives you the greatest sense of satisfaction? What rewards are available to you? What is the culmination of your contribution?

Health

Consider your health. Imagine the kind of health you want for yourself. Include emotional, physical, mental, and spiritual health in your vision. Imagine how you will maintain a healthy life. What kind of activities and thoughts can help you achieve and continue your vision of health?

Enriching Activities

Now look at personal hobbies, adventures, and volunteer involvements that fulfill your other aspirations. Imagine having all the enjoyable, satisfying, and contributing aspects of your life in your vision. What do you bring to these activities? What do they contribute to enriching and rounding out your life?

After you have considered these questions and answered them in a form that is most comfortable for you, take a look at the whole. How do all the pieces fit together? What does the complete vision look like? Are there aspects that are in conflict with one another? Does your vision create a coherent whole? Does it please and inspire you? Is it a vision worth your commitment and energy? In the space opposite, write your vision for your own life.

Your Vision for Yourself

. . . .
. . . .
. . . .
. . . .
. . . .
. . . .
. . . .
. . . .
. . . .
. . . .
. . . .
. . . .
. . . .
. . . .
. . . .
. . . .
. . . .
. . . .
. . . .
. . . .
. . . .
. . . .
. . . .
. . . .

Communication and Your Vision—An Exercise

Your vision will be a powerful force for change only if it is communicated to others in ways that are accessible and inspiring to them. The first step in transforming a dream into reality is communicating your vision to others.

Communicating your vision requires attention and conscious planning. We often communicate as though we are talking to a mirror image of ourselves, not realizing that those we intend to inspire have different concerns from our own. Leaders must understand their followers, and followers must understand those who lead. Former Senator John Tunney of California described Robert Kennedy's ability to create a magical connection with those he wished to reach:

> His sense of politics was physical, in that he knew you had to throw your-
> self out there among the people again and again, to be directly heard and
> seen and touched and sort of handled and pushed around by them. There's
> a huge hunger to connect to an actual physical presence—a tribal leader,
> really, with that kind of personal relationship between him and the peo-
> ple—who can give them a sense of meaning and value as a community
> again. It's something almost primitive, mystic.

Both John and Robert Kennedy were brilliant at translating their visions into a physical presence and vivid language that enabled each of us to be touched by them. We were willing to follow their dream because they made it real for us.

In this exercise you will try to capture this mystic quality for yourself by working with your organizational vision. Your challenge will be to communicate it powerfully and with inspiration so that others embrace and support it. Tunney describes how Robert Kennedy "has almost recklessly, with a willingness to take extraordinary risks, given himself over completely to what he believes in, which answers what they believe in." Your presentation of your vision should have the following qualities: It should express your excitement, love for, and commitment to your dream; it should be brief yet full; it should be clear and vivid.

In presenting your vision, make it engaging and inspiring, perhaps by using drawings, a song, poetry, a skit, or a narrative story so that you involve others. In planning your presentation, think about your audience and speak to what will fire them up, reach their hearts, excite them with your dream.

Here you have an opportunity to develop your communication skills. If you have been working alone, invite a small group of colleagues or friends to assist you. Invite them to hear or see your vision and discuss it with you. Let them know that you really value their reactions. Set the stage by asking them to set aside their view of today's reality and visit the future with you. If you are already in a small group or part of a larger one, continue with this group as your vision partners.

Our object is to give you an opportunity to communicate your vision for the organization in such a way that others can feel inspired and excited about it. If others in your group have also created a vision for the organization, have them present their vision to the others.

A. After the presentation(s), the tendency will be for everyone to want to discuss *what the vision said.* Try to postpone that conversation and first focus on *how* it was communicated.

B. Notice the differences in each person's communication. Elicit feedback about what was effective or problematic about each presentation.

C. Now discuss the substance of the vision(s). If several were presented for the same organization, notice the differences and discuss the basis of each difference.

D. Look for commonalities in everyone's vision statement. Try to create a group vision for the future of the organization. This exercise can be a team-building activity in which everyone shares a common vision.

E. If you are the only person with a vision, work with the group so they can see it as their own. Have them discuss the parts of the vision they like and suggest changes in parts that do not satisfy them.

F. Discuss making a presentation of your vision to a special group in the organization: a group of clients, managers, secretaries, or outside vendors. How would you change your communication to speak to these specific interest groups?

As others work with your vision statement you will need to allow others to change it. Do not get defensive. Let them make it theirs. Stay true to your basic principles but let them rework the language and ideas so that everyone can buy in to it. Jim Burke, chairman and CEO of Johnson & Johnson, spends 40 percent of his time communicating the Johnson & Johnson credo. More than 800 managers have attended J&J challenge meetings, where they go through General Johnson's credo line by line to see what changes they feel need to be made. Over the years some of these changes have been fundamental. Like the U.S. Constitution, the essence of the credo endures.

Learning to Lead

As a final step in the visioning process, or if you do not feel ready to present your personal vision to colleagues, share it with those closest to you. Talk to your family about your dreams for life in the future. See how your personal vision compares with your organizational vision. Is there dissonance between the two? Ask your friends and family for their reactions and support. Let them create a vision for themselves. Allow your vision to become theirs or have theirs integrated into yours.

Jesse Jackson, a master visionary and communicator, describes his early evolution as he began to share his dreams with others. In a *New Yorker* magazine portrait of this complex, riveting orator by Marshall Frady, Jackson talks about how he learned to create a vision that reached the hearts of others.

> When I first came back home from the seminary, I was asked to speak at church, and my grandmother and some of the older folk came up afterward. "That was a nice speech, young man, very nice speech." They meant the words were. Words came out nice. That's what it was, a speech. But as you go on and begin to really catch hold of it, you start hearing them say, "Well, now. You spoke to my soul. You burned me this morning." Got to do more than *speak*. You can get informed listening to a newsman or weatherman. You got to be moving toward the heart of the matter, got to burn people's souls. You got to get *inside* of people. That's where it all is. And you can't get inside of them unless you open *yourself* up to be got inside *of*. Follow what I'm saying? The key to other people's hearts is finding the key to yours. Got to give to receive, got to open up yourself to get inside somebody else.
>
> (Marshall Frady, *New Yorker*)

Jackson's lesson is that as we create and communicate the visions from our heart, we powerfully connect with those we want to join us in realizing our dreams. Bringing our vision into reality is the next test for a leader. In Chapter Six you will learn to create the trusting relationships between leaders and followers that transform our visions into reality.

Chapter 6

Maintaining Trust through Integrity

In which we understand how to build trust through vision, empathy, consistency, and integrity; create our code of ethics and discover our integrity gap.

This story shall the good man teach his son;
And Crispin Crispin shall ne'er go by,
From this day to the ending of the world,
But we in it shall be remembered;
We few, we happy few, we band of brothers;
For he to-day that sheds his blood with me
Shall be my brother; be he ne'er so vile,
This day shall gentle his condition:
And gentlemen in England now a-bed
Shall think themselves accursed they were not
    here,
And hold their manhoods cheap whiles any
    speaks
That fought with us upon Saint Crispin's day.

William Shakespeare, *Life of King Henry V*

Trust and Organizational Effectiveness

Why did young and old follow Harry into the bloody battle of Agincourt? Why did India's poor march to the sea with Gandhi against the salt tax? What was it about Margaret Sanger that emboldened women to break with husbands and family and adopt birth control? We

119

know that each of these leaders believed in the rightness of their cause at a moment in history when action was called for. But their impact was felt because of the trust these leaders enjoyed, trust that was based on their invincible integrity and powerful commitment. Trust is the essential quality that creates a following for the leaders in which we are most interested. It is the secret of their ability to inspire those who create movements for social change and build the organizations that realize their dreams.

Trust provides the motivation and energy that makes it possible for organizations to work. It is hard to imagine an institution without some semblance of trust operating somewhere. It is what motivates heroism, sells products, and keeps communication humming. Trust is the source of organizational integrity. Like leadership, trust is hard to describe, let alone define. We know when it is present and we know when it is not. We are aware that it is essential and that it is based on predictability. We trust people who are predictable, whose positions are known and who keep at it; leaders who are trusted make themselves known and make their positions clear. Organizations without trust would resemble the nightmare of Kafka's *Castle,* where nothing can be certain and no one can be relied on or held accountable. The ability to predict outcomes with a high probability of success generates and maintains trust.

In this chapter we explore trust by focusing on four qualities of leadership that, when practiced, engender trust. They are vision, empathy, consistency, and integrity. A leader who is trusted demonstrates these four characteristics.

- The leader has a *vision* for the organization that is clear, attractive, and attainable. We tend to trust leaders who create inspiring visions. The leader's vision functions as a context that provides shared beliefs and a common organizational purpose with which we can identify and feel that we belong. The leader involves us in the vision, empowers us to create it, and communicates the shared vision so that we integrate it into our lives.

- The leader has unconditional *empathy* for those who live in the organization. We tend to trust leaders who can walk in our shoes and are able to let us know that, although they may have a different point of view, they are able to see the world as we see it and understand the sense we make of it.

- The leader's positions are *consistent.* We tend to trust leaders when we know where they stand in relation to the organization and how they position the organization relative to the environment. We understand how our leaders' positions evolved and know that they are willing to reconsider them in the face of new evidence.

- The leader's *integrity* is unquestionable. We tend to trust leaders who stand for a higher moral order and who demonstrate their ethical commitments through actions that we can observe. Leaders uphold a standard of ethics and call themselves and others to account for deviations from this moral code.

Qualities of Leadership—An Exercise

We begin with an exercise that will enable you to explore and make explicit your experiences with the four qualities associated with trust. As you may remember from our work in earlier chapters, we believe that self-reflection and awareness are the key to our lifelong ability to learn. Encouraging others to trust us requires personal action. It is not something an organization can mandate a person to do. In becoming a leader, you will want to commit yourself to being trustworthy and aligning your actions with your commitment. Reflection is the initial step in the process. It permits you to acknowledge your feelings, understand them, resolve your questions, and get on with your work. In this case your work is to win and maintain the trust of others.

The purpose of this exercise is to reflect on the qualities of leadership that elicit trust. To begin, refer back to Chapter One and the list of leaders that you identified in your life.

A. Review your list and add the names of others you have noticed since you began working in your workbook. Eliminate the people you have come to consider managers rather than leaders. Number each person so you can place them on the diagram below.

B. The diagram on page 123 is a *socio-gram* that graphs social relationships. Begin by placing yourself at the center of the hub. Now add the names of leaders on the spokes coming out from the hub. The length of each spoke indicates the social distance between yourself and the particular leader designated by the spoke. For example, if you consider Gloria Steinem an important leader in your life and do not know her personally, put her on a spoke that is a greater distance from the center, such as Leader #4. If one of the leaders on your list is the man who leads your son's Boy Scout troop and you consider him a close friend, place him close to you (for instance, as Leader #2). If you consider yourself a leader, put a number for yourself on the chart at the hub.

C. Reflect upon the social distance of each person in the diagram from your position at the hub. What do you notice about the relationship between your position and others and among the various leaders on the chart? Are there any surprises? Do you notice any patterns? Observe the distance of leaders from you at the hub. Are these distances associated with gender, race, age, social class, or role?

D. Next, add the qualities of leadership that engender trust to the chart. In the space on the diagram beside each leader's number place the following designations:

a *V* for those who have and express an inspiring personal and professional vision;

an *E* for those who demonstrate the ability to empathize;

a *P* for those leaders who have clear and consistent positions and use them to orient the organization;

an *I* for those leaders who demonstrate integrity through ethical practices.

For example, if former Secretary of Defense Clark Clifford, long considered an American leader, were on your list, he might have a *V* for being a visionary, and a *P* for consistency of positions for himself and his organizations. But with his involvement in the BCCI banking scandal, he might not have an *I* for integrity, or perhaps not an *E* for empathizing with the people who lost their savings because of the banks dealings.

On the other hand, if Marian Wright Edelman, founder of the Children's Defense Fund and long-time advocate for children in poverty, were on your list, she might have all four letters next to her name. Your chart might look like the one on the next page.

E. Reflect on your chart. What do you notice? Who are the leaders with integrity? Is there a pattern regarding leaders with vision? Are the leaders located closer to you the ones who express empathy?

F. Notice the relationships among the leaders on your chart. Can you connect lines between leaders who know each other? Do you notice any patterns among them? Who are the leaders who are related? Do they have characteristics in common?

G. If you are working with a group, share your socio-gram with others. You need not mention names if you used numbers and would rather not reveal the identity of those on your diagram. Discuss the patterns you noticed with your group members. If you are willing to share names, discuss whether some members of your group have the same people on your charts or placed them in different positions with different assessments.

Socio-Gram of Social Relations with Leaders

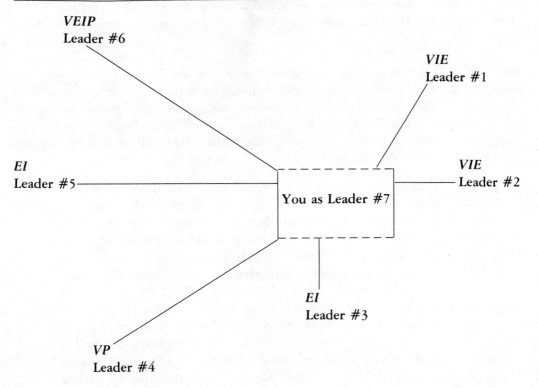

H. What do you notice about trust? Who are the leaders on your chart that you trust the most? What are the characteristics that matter to you? Do you trust someone more if they empathize with you, or is their integrity more important to you? What does this exercise tell you about your own values?

As we continue our exploration of trust we will investigate the concepts of vision, empathy, consistency, and integrity in greater depth. You may want to return to this socio-gram to refine your views of the leaders in your life.

Support through Empathy

As you will recall, we addressed creating and communicating a vision in Chapter Five. You may want to review your work to remind yourself of the power of an articulated vision. A basic ingredient of leadership is having a guiding vision. Leaders who are trusted have a clear idea of what they want to do professionally and personally—and the strength to persist in realizing this dream in the face of setbacks, even failures. Having a clear vision reminds us that unless we know where we are going and why, we cannot possibly get there. As the Greek philosopher Heraclitus wrote: "If we do not expect the unexpected it will never happen."

With only a vision, many leaders end up not being prophets, but frustrated, lonely, and ineffectual failures. Leaders cannot achieve their dreams without getting people on their side. How do they do that? Ultimately, leaders' abilities to galvanize their co-workers resides both in their understanding of themselves and their co-workers needs and wants, along with their belief in their mission. Sydney Pollack described the leader's ability to bring people onto his side this way:

> Up to a point, I think you can lead out of fear, intimidation, as awful as that sounds. You can make people follow you by scaring them, and you can make people follow by having them feel obligated. You can lead by creating guilt. There is a lot of leadership that comes out of fear depen-dence, and guilt. The marine boot camp is famous for it. But the problem is that you're creating obedience with a residue of resentment. If you want to make a physics analogy, you'd be moving through the medium but you'd be creating a lot of drag, a lot of backwash. There are two other qualities that I think are more positive reasons to follow someone. One is an honest belief in the person you're following. The other is selfish. The person following has to believe that following is the best thing to do at the time. I mean it has to be apparent to them that they are getting something better by following you than they ever would by not following you. You don't want people to follow you just because that's what they're paid for. Sometimes you can teach them something. "You're going to learn more by doing this movie than you would by doing another movie" let's say. You try to make everyone feel they have a stake in it.

Visionary leaders enable people to feel they have a stake in it. They empower them to experience the vision as their own. They offer people opportunities to create their own vision, to explore what the vision will mean to their jobs and lives, and to envision their future as part of the vision for the organization. They have the ability to reach out to others and see them as separate from themselves, but also, in some deeper sense, to know that they are alike. We call this ability empathy.

Dr. Norman Paul, a national leader in the field of family therapy, believes empathy is a key to successful family life. In his essay "Parental Empathy" he presents observations about empathy in a family context. They are appropriate for leadership empathy in organizational life as well.

> An empathizer, or subject, accepts, for a brief period, the object's total emotional individuality, not only his simple emotions but his whole state of being—the history of his desires, feelings, and thoughts as well as other forces and experiences that are expressed in his behavior. The object senses the emphathizer's response and realizes that for a brief point in time the two have fused. If he then takes the initiative of communicating more of his experience and feelings, he provides a basic stimulus for what can become a mutual empathic process.
>
> Empathy is different from sympathy; the two processes are, in fact, mutually exclusive. In sympathy, the subject is principally absorbed in his own feelings as they are projected into the object and has little concern for the reality and validity of the object's special experience. Sympathy bypasses real understanding of the other person, and that other is denied his own sense of being. Empathy, on the other hand, presupposes the existence of the object as a separate individual, entitled to his own feelings, ideas and emotional history. The empathizer makes no judgments about what the other *should* feel, but solicits the expression of whatever he *does* feel and, for brief periods, experiences these feelings as his own. The empathizer oscillates between such subjective involvement and a detached recognition of the shared feelings. The periods of his objective detachment do not seem to the other to be spells of indifference, as they would in sympathy; they are, instead, evidence that the subject respects himself and the object as separate people. Secure in his sense of self and his own emotional boundaries, the empathizer attempts to nurture a similar security in the other.
>
> (Norman Paul, "Parental Empathy")

Most of us know when a leader with whom we interact empathizes with us. We experience being understood on a deep level. It feels as though we are more than understood, we are *known*. But empathetic leaders do not merge with us. They do not take away our feelings or responses. They do not overpower us with their resonance. An empathetic leader acknowledges our position and walks in our shoes.

The Practice of Empathy—An Exercise

Learning to empathize calls for a conscious effort to listen to the other person and hear what they are saying in the context of their own orientation, needs, and perceptions. Empathizing requires having your attention on the other person rather than inside on yourself. Letting the other person know you empathize with their situation, their position, their feelings means:

- feeding back to them what you hear them say or see them do;
- asking them questions to learn more about what they really feel or believe;
- repeating their comments as you hear them without adding your own ideas; and
- understanding their point of view from the inside, as though it were your own.

An empathic leader does not judge the responses of others or crowd them with the leader's agenda, but gives them silence and space to have their own reactions, and lets them know that they have been heard.

In this exercise you will have an opportunity to practice skills in empathy. It is easy to empathize with someone you like, someone with whom you identify or someone who is taking a position you admire. It is more difficult to practice empathy with someone who creates problems and is disagreeable. The following is a case study of a difficult subject. In reading his story, you may not like what he says or does. You make find yourself getting annoyed or exasperated. Here is a test of empathy—see if you can understand him as though it were you.

Our case study is the story of Ed. We would like you to read his history from the perspective of his boss, Baxter, someone who needs and wants to empathize with Ed so he can support him in learning new behavior. Try to get underneath and behind his behavior. Find a place in yourself from which you can know him. After reading the case, complete the exercise.

> Ed was born of working-class parents in Brooklyn, New York. Smart, ambitious, determined to succeed, he went to work in a factory right out of high school and enrolled in night school. Working day and night, he managed to take a degree in accounting. He moved off the factory floor and into management with the same manufacturing firm. In a few short years, he fought his way up the ladder, passing some MBAs on the way. He proved himself to be not only hardworking and aggressive, but a talented nuts-and-bolts man. Efficient, competent, and tough, he was eventually made a vice president.

Ed was a company man. Everyone said so. He not only knew how everything worked, he was capable of making it work better, and when necessary, he didn't mind yanking out the deadwood. He was not an easy man to work for, but he was just the kind of man his bosses liked. He lacked the skills to communicate with those who worked for him. You never heard a "well done" or "good job," you only heard complaints. He was 100 percent loyal to the company, a workaholic, always willing and eager to go that extra mile and impatient with anyone who was less devoted than he.

Ed's competence, combined with his drive and toughness, made him an ideal executive in the win-or-die 1980s. To look at him or see him in action, no one would ever have guessed that he grew up poor on the streets of South Brooklyn, or that he was a night-school product.

In fact, he'd nearly forgotten it himself. He looked, dressed, and talked like his bosses. He had an attractive, devoted wife who looked, dressed, and talked like his bosses' wives. He had two handsome, well-behaved sons, a nice house in Westchester, a wicked tennis serve, and great prospects—if he wanted to move. The president of his company was in his early fifties, Ed's age, and was happy with his position, seeing no room at the top for Ed in the foreseeable future.

About the time Ed began getting restless, a family-owned firm in the same industry was looking for new blood. The CEO, the grandson of the founder, was thinking of retirement, and there was no one to whom he could hand over the reins. He wanted to bring someone in as a vice president, get to know him, and if all went well, turn the firm over to him within two or three years. Although the firm was based in Minneapolis, the executive search firm found Ed in New York. Ed saw the move to Minneapolis as his shortcut to the top.

He handled the job-hop as efficiently as he handled everything else. He moved his family into a bigger and better house in Edina, moved himself into a big corner office with a view of a lake, and seemed to adjust to the slower Midwestern rhythm without missing a beat.

But he was, if anything, tougher than before, coming down harder than ever on people who failed to please him. He often exploded, giving vent to his anger and he was known to blame others for his own mistakes. The more relaxed Minnesotans in the office made fun of him privately, nick-named him "the Brooklyn Bomber," but when he said jump, they jumped.

After Ed had been in Minneapolis about a year, Baxter, the CEO, took him to lunch and offered him the COO (Chief Operating Officer) spot. Ed was pleased but not surprised. No one worked harder than he did, no one could have learned more about the company than he had, and no one de-served it more. The sky was the limit for the Bomber now. Baxter and Ed were a great team. Baxter, genial and encouraging, steered the company, while Ed, tougher than ever, took care of the nuts and bolts, the dirty work.

Baxter decided that Ed was indeed the fellow to replace him when he retired, and he announced his decision to the family—who were also the board of directors. For the first time in his life, Ed ran into something he couldn't tough his way through. Some members of the family board told Baxter that Ed was *too* tough, too rough on his fellow executives. They would not approve his appointment unless Ed improved his "people skills."

Baxter gave Ed the bad news. If Ed was disturbed—and he was—so was the CEO. Baxter was ready to retire, and further, he'd chosen Ed as his successor and had begun to groom him for the job. Now his orderly plan had fallen apart.

After a while, it became clear that everything everyone said about Ed was true. He was very competent and very ambitious, but he was also a tyrant. He was impulsive and frequently abusive of people who worked for him. They would actually cower in his presence. He had a desperate need to control both people and events. He was incapable of thanking anyone for a job well done—he couldn't even give a compliment. Also, he was a sexist and did not treat the women who worked under him as professionals.

Your task in this exercise is to counsel Ed on what he should do to recoup his position or develop a satisfactory alternate strategy. To be useful to Ed and successful in advising him, you must first empathize with him and his situation. The following questions may help you:

Chapter 6—Maintaining Trust through Integrity

Questions to Consider

A. What are Ed's insecurities and fears? Where do they come from?

....

....

....

....

B. What has he contributed to the company in the past?

....

....

....

....

C. What personal price has he paid to play the game by the rules as he perceived them?

....

....

....

....

D. How does Ed feel now that his climb to the top has been thwarted?

....

....

....

....

E. What are the questions he is raising for himself as his game plan unravels?

....

....

....

....

Learning to Lead

As you reflect on Ed's situation, try to empathize with him. When have you had a similar experience in your life? How did you feel? What did you do with those feelings? How did others react? How do you think he is feeling when he receives the news from Baxter about the board's decision?

Create a scenario for a counseling session with Ed. If you are working with a group, you may want to set up a role play in which you play Ed's boss or consultant and someone else (the person who most dislikes Ed) plays Ed. This experience will give the person playing Ed a greater opportunity to empathize.

If you are working alone, write out your dialogue. In writing you will want to play both parts: yours, as the boss/consultant, and Ed's, as the advisee. This exercise will enable you to see the world from Ed's point of view.

Counseling Session Notes

. . . .

. . . .

. . . .

. . . .

. . . .

. . . .

. . . .

. . . .

. . . .

Stages in the Empathic Interview
Introducing the Session

Begin by creating an introduction to the conversation with Ed. Tell him why you are here and what you intend to achieve from the counseling session. Assume that he is willing to work with you. Since he remains in character, however, he feels he needs to be tough and to let you know that he knows it all.

Setting the Stage

Create an opportunity for Ed to tell you what is wrong. As he speaks, empathize with his feelings. Try to see the situation from his point of view. Give him the opportunity to speak his mind and heart by remaining silent but encouraging with nods and body language.

Giving Empathic Remarks

Let him know that you can appreciate his situation and his feelings. Show him through summarizing and acknowledgment that you empathize with him. Encourage him to explore the issues further. Let him know you are with him in the search for a solution. Create a partnership with him.

Providing Supportive Feedback

Give Ed some honest feedback on his behavior and point of view. Let him know you are speaking from his self interest and that of the company. Give him direct responses. Do not protect him from himself. Be straight with him but supportive at the same time. Ask him if he is willing to try to improve his communication skills. If he resists, let him know again that you empathize by reflecting back to him some of his own comments. See if he can express empathy for others or understand why his behavior upset them.

Soliciting Reactions

Find out from Ed how he is receiving your feedback. Hear what he has to say, and if it is critical of you, use this as an opportunity to model how to accept criticism. Listen for his disappointment, pain, and sense of failure. Let him know you hear these feelings and that you can understand why he might feel that way. If you are getting lost in Ed's problems, reread Norman Paul's definition of empathy to center yourself.

Eliciting Changes

Help Ed to create his own plan of action. Focus on what he can do to change. Ask him to come up with a game plan for new behavior. Ask him to indicate the changes he would like to see in how others treat him. Prompt him to say what he will do differently to elicit new behavior and attitudes from others.

Offering Acknowledgment

Thank Ed for taking the risk of being open to himself and to you. Let him see how courageous he was to be willing to change. Empathize with what it took for him to observe himself and identify the changes he will need to make to stimulate a different response from others.

Learning to Lead

In earlier chapters we asked you to be self-reflective, to observe your behavior and learn from what you see. Use these skills again here. Notice how you felt when you empathized with Ed. What were the problems? What was it about him that triggered a reaction in you? The issues you have with Ed and your difficulties in empathizing with him provide information about your own difficulties with yourself. The buttons that Ed pushed by his attitudes and behaviors represent incomplete or unresolved concerns you have with yourself. The people with whom we cannot empathize represent the unconscious or hidden dislikes we have about ourselves. These people are our greatest teachers.

On the left side of a piece of paper make a list of the people with whom you are unable to empathize. Leave space between each name. On the right side of the paper, list the attributes of each person that you find disagreeable or that block your empathy with them. Now review the list of attributes and notice the similarities. These attributes or characteristics may be the ones you do not like in yourself or are afraid you have, and so avoid them. If you want to be more effective in empathizing with others, these are the problems to confront in yourself. By accepting them as part of your own make-up, you will be able to tolerate them in the other person. Then you will be able to empathize with them and have more productive relationships with them.

Leaders must be self-directed and self-reflective, listening to their inner voice and taking direction from their values and vision. But learning and understanding are the keys to self-direction, and it is through our relationships with others that we learn about ourselves. Empathy is our greatest teacher about others and about ourselves. As Boris Pasternak wrote in *Doctor Zhivago*,

> Well, what are you? What is it about you that you have always known as yourself? What are you conscious of in yourself: your kidneys, your liver, your blood vessels? No. However far back you go in your memory it is always some external manifestation of yourself where you come across your identity: in the work of your hands, in your family, in other people. And now, listen carefully. You in others—this is what you are, this is what your consciousness has breathed, and lived on, and enjoyed throughout your life, your soul, your immortality—your life in others.
>
> (Boris Pasternak, *Doctor Zhivago*)

Trust through Consistent Integrity

Ten years ago, *Time* magazine's cover story asked, "What Ever Happened to Ethics? Assaulted by sleaze, scandals and hypocrisy, America searches for its moral bearings." The editors went on to say:

. . . at a time of moral disarray, America seeks to rebuild a structure of values. . . . Large sections of the nation's ethical roofing have been sagging badly, from the White House to churches, schools, industries, medical centers, law firms, and stock brokerages—pressing down on the institutions and enterprises that make up the body and blood of America. At the same time, the collapse of standards brings ethical issues to the forefront. Many Americans feel a need to start rebuilding the edifice, to re-evaluate the basis of public morality. In so doing, says Joseph Kockelmans, professor of philosophy at Pennsylvania State University, "people may finally begin to take responsibility for their lives, instead of just being sheep."

This country desperately needs leaders who consistently express a moral and ethical integrity. We have become numb to scandal and corruption in high places. Although it may not be condoned, it is definitely expected. Trust of our leaders has been abandoned. Cynicism has taken its place. How do we re-establish trust? We must develop leaders who express a clear and compelling vision, who consistently demonstrate empathy, and who can be counted on to practice ethical patterns of behavior. It is consistent integrity that we are seeking, tried and true ethical action. It is reliability, or what we prefer to call constancy.

A recent national study indicates that people would much rather follow individuals they can count on even when they disagree with their viewpoint, than people whose viewpoint they agree with but who flip-flop in getting there, or who could change at any time. We cannot emphasize enough the significance of constancy and, if you will, staying the course. A leader's regular and consistent pattern provides security and builds trust. This pattern must reflect strong moral and ethical values for trust to fully blossom between a leader and followers. Leaders generate and sustain trust by exemplifying:

Constancy
Whatever surprises leaders themselves face, they do not create any for the group. They maintain continuity and security.

Congruity
Leaders walk their talk. There is no gap between the theories they espouse and the ones they practice. Their morality is found in their behavior.

Reliability
Leaders are there when it counts; they are ready to support their co-workers in the moments that matter.

Integrity

Leaders honor their commitments and promises. They are ethical in their relationships.

Harold Williams, president of the J. Paul Getty Trust, gets at this when he describes his first experiences as chairman of the Securities and Exchange Commission (SEC):

> If there is anything I feel good about [at the Commission], it's the way I came through in terms of my own personal values and my personal self. If you believe in your course, you gotta stay with it in terms of course and timing. I think it's tough at times—when the press are all over you and you start hearing from Capitol Hill and you know that even some of your own staff are feeding the stories and the corporate community is up in arms, and there were several times when it was all going that way and it gets kind of heavy. . . . But if you believe you're right, and you've got your own integrity—and I think that's where it really ends up—I mean: "Do you believe in what you're doing?"—And if you believe it you stay with it. I couldn't change course and still respect myself.

But in an environment that best-selling author and management consultant Tom Peters describes as chaotic, where change is the only constant, how can a leader maintain consistent positions without seeming to be rigid and unresponsive to shifting realities? It is a fine line to walk in today's volatile climate to steer a clear and consistent course while empathizing, responding, and dealing with change. Leaders are expected to acknowledge uncertainties and deal effectively with the present, while simultaneously anticipating and responding to the future. This means endlessly expressing, explaining, extending, expanding, and when necessary revising the organization's mission and their own vision. Leaders can change their minds, but they need to be consistent in their openness to change, how they communicate these changes, how they behave in relation to change, and how they explain the thinking process that took them to a new position.

Thomas L. Friedman, writing in the *New York Times* about President Clinton, then in office one month, describes his problem of constancy as follows:

> How will Mr. Clinton respond when the screaming starts? One friend of Mr. Clinton compares him to a character in the television show "Star Trek: The Next Generation." The character is an "Empath," one of a race of people born with an ability to empathize with and absorb the feelings of

others. As he prepares his economic program, the Empath President is clearly uneasy. "More than anything else he doesn't want to anger people," said the friend. "He wants to be loved. He doesn't want to do things that will hurt people, but that is fundamentally incompatible with the Presidency."

Clinton, like all of us, wants to be loved. Staying the course, maintaining a consistent focus, and being predictable in terms of what he believes may not always lead to love, but will lead to effective leadership through trust.

We are not advocating that leaders take a position and stick to it no matter what. In today's organizations, which require flexible, responsive, innovative leadership, digging in one's heels and sticking to one's guns are strategies that are doomed to failure. But we *are* urging constancy in ethics and integrity. Leaders are responsible for the set of ethics and norms that govern the behavior of people in the organization. Leaders can lead through ethics in several ways. One is to demonstrate by their own behavior their commitment to the ethics they are trying to institutionalize. Leaders set the moral tone by carefully choosing the people with whom they surround themselves, by communicating a sense of purpose to the organization, by reinforcing appropriate behavior, and by articulating moral positions to external and internal constituencies. John Gardner, writing in *No Easy Victories,* describes a leader's role with regard to ethics as follows:

> Leaders have a significant role in creating the state of mind that is the society. They can serve as symbols of the moral unity of the society. They can express the values that hold the society together. Most important, they can conceive and articulate goals that lift people out of their petty preoccupations, carry them above the conflicts that tear a society apart, and unite them in pursuit of objectives worthy of their best efforts.

In the end, vision, empathy, constancy, and integrity are all different faces of a common property of leadership—the ability to integrate in trusting relationships those who act with what must be done, so all work together as a single organism in harmony with itself and its niche in the environment.

Your Ethical Ten Commandments—An Exercise

One of the most powerful archetypes of a leader in western culture is Moses, whose leadership was founded in his ability to move people to action with a vision of freedom and the promised land. He was as troubled by the corruption of his time as we are today. His response was to deliver the Ten Commandments, a code of ethics by which they had to live in order to achieve their vision.

When we speak of a code of ethics and integrity, we mean standards of moral and intellectual honesty on which conduct is based. Without integrity we betray ourselves and others and cheapen every endeavor. It is the single quality whose absence we feel most sharply on every level of our national life. But the nation's integrity will be restored only when each of us asserts our own integrity. By their very existence, people of integrity lend hope to our innate conviction that as a people, we can rise above the current moral cynicism and squalor. As Aristotle wrote in *Ethics,* "If you would understand virtue, observe the conduct of virtuous men."

The current rash of scandals is the sum of millions of undiscovered, uncounted cheatings, evasions, cover-ups, half truths, and moral erosions, not only in our leaders, but in the whole society. The slogan for these seedy times is "Everybody does it." Integrity, like charity, begins at home.

In this exercise you are asked to take an honest look at your own code of ethics. Using the metaphor of the Ten Commandments, we invite you to write your own moral and ethical standards for behavior. This is an opportunity to scan your belief system to discover your values, your ethics, your code for your own behavior and that of others. It is one thing to hold a set of moral values and another to live by them. The true test of a leader's integrity is the consistent expression of a code of ethics in action. Our ability to know what we believe and our commitment to live by those beliefs are necessary to create relationships of trust with those we work with.

In this exercise you will need to work alone at the beginning, and later with others. Complete the following charts by practicing self-reflection and observing your own behavior. You will notice that on the first chart you are asked to create your Ten Commandments for ethics in your organization. These commandments are the ten most important values you hold for your work. On the second chart, indicate a behavior you have demonstrated that exemplifies the commandment. For example, if one of your commandments is to "do no work that contributes to the loss of life of another human being," you might have a practice that evaluates the products manufactured by your company to make sure there is no toxic waste being dumped where humans can be harmed. If you have a commandment that says "never cheat the company out of money," you might have a behavior that checks your expense reports for accuracy and honesty.

The Ten Commandments for Ethics on the Job

1.
   ....

2.
   ....

3.
   ....

4.
   ....

5.
   ....

6.
   ....

7.
   ....

8.
   ....

9.
   ....

10.
   ....

Behaviors Consistent with Each Commandment

1.
....

2.
....

3.
....

4.
....

5.
....

6.
....

7.
....

8.
....

9.
....

10.
....

....

After you have completed these charts on your own, share them with others. It would be useful to share your commandments with colleagues at work to see the similarities and differences that might exist. Notice the primary focus of each person.

Questions to Consider

A. What do you care most about and how do you express your values?

B. Which commandments are most difficult to use as guides for action?

C. Were there any commandments that are important to you but to which you could not find any corresponding behaviors?

D. If you and your colleagues know each other, give each other feedback about whether your behavior matches your commandments.

E. What have you and your colleagues noticed about each other and your willingness to take a stand for your values?

F. How does your organization support you in following your commandments, and how does it hinder you?

The Integrity Gap—An Exercise

There is often a gap between what we believe is right and the actions we take. Melissa Everett, Dr. John Mack, and Dr. Robert Oresick are authors of a study that addresses the stresses and conflicts faced by corporate executives as they try to increase profit and improve company products while remaining true to their moral and ethical commitments. In *Re-Inventing the Corporate Self: The Inner Agenda for Business Transformation,* a study of their research, they found two types of executives, those they called "principled risk takers" and those they characterized as "conventional decision makers." They analyzed their interviews of twenty-four senior executives in publicly held corporations and discovered differences in three areas:

1. Self-Consistency: Wholeness or Compartmentalization

Did individuals see life as an integrated whole in which their beliefs applied to work as well as to church groups, volunteer organizations, and values at home?

2. Personal Efficacy: High or Limited Sense of Agency

Did individuals have a sense of power and control in their work life so that they believed they could take action to express their values?

3. Scope of Awareness: Global or Circumscribed

Did individuals see themselves as global citizens with responsibilities that are larger than their own corner of the world?

Learning to Lead

In this exercise you will need a partner. Your partner's job is to interview you by asking questions that will enable you to discover where you stand with regard to being a "principled risk taker" or "conventional decision maker."

No one is completely one type or another. We are all combinations of both. But this exercise will let you know where you stand in terms of your own "integrity gap," so you can make informed choices about your actions in relation to your commandments.

The interviewer begins by asking the questions below. If you think of other questions, add them to the list. She or he will write down your responses and give them to you for analysis. *Do not* think long and hard about each answer, but respond quickly and accurately. When you have completed the interview, change roles and you become the interviewer. When you have both been interviewed, read over your responses and share your observations and realizations with each other.

Interview Questions

A. When you come to work, do you feel you have to put aside ethical values that are important to you in order to get along and be successful? If so, what are they?

....

....

....

....

B. Have you ever experienced a situation at work when you knew the right action to take but felt you should or could not take it because it would not be accepted or valued? If so, please describe.

....

....

....

....

C. Are there activities at home or outside of work in which you act on moral values that you wish you could express at work? Are there feelings you have when you volunteer for a community organization or church group that you do not have at work but would like to have? If so, what are they?

....
....
....
....

D. Do you feel you have the authority and power to act on beliefs that are important to you at work? If so, what actions have you taken to express your values?

....
....
....
....

E. Are you aware of your organization's impact on the larger community, and on the world as a whole? If so, is this impact positive, negative, or a complex picture? Please describe it.

....
....
....
....

F. How does your work contribute to the forward movement of your society, of people in other societies and the world as a whole? If you do not see a connection to the larger community, what impact does your work have on your local community?

....
....
....
....

G. Do you see yourself as a global citizen with responsibilities for people and events beyond your community and your country? If so, what are some examples of your responsibilities? If not, how do you see yourself relating to people and events in the world beyond your community?

. . . .

. . . .

. . . .

. . . .

When you and your partner have completed the interviews and analysis of your responses, you will have a picture of your integrity gap. In the next chapter we will learn how to create a plan of action to increase the congruence between your values and your actions. The trust of a leader grows directly out of the consistent expression of ethics through communication and action. Dr. Martin Luther King, Jr., writing from a Birmingham jail, speaks of the responsibility of each of us to live out our beliefs in action:

> I am coming to feel that the people of ill will have used time much more effectively than the people of good will. We will have to repent in this generation not merely for the vitriolic works and actions of the bad people, but for the appalling silence of the good people. We must come to see that human progress never rolls in on wheels of inevitability. It comes through the tireless efforts and persistent work of men willing to be co-workers with God, and without this hard work itself becomes an ally of the forces of social stagnation. We must use time creatively, and forever realize that the time is always ripe to do right.
>
> (Martin Luther King, Jr.)

Chapter 7

Realizing Intention through Action

In which we examine what it takes for leaders to translate their vision into action, affirm the essentials of being a leader, and investigate goals, commitment, power, and strategic thinking as they enable us to act.

In all we do, we must affirm an unyielding moral vision—that the next generation is entitled to participate fully in reinventing and benefiting from the American future. If we believe in ourselves, we will find and create a vital and participatory community in which every student, faculty, and staff member is valued and respected, in which we recognize that we share common values as educated and ethical human beings, and in which the bonds of community are stronger than the habits of cultural ignorance. That is our fervent goal.

If we believe in ourselves, we will create the kind of learning environment and campus community that will prepare our graduates for a lifetime of learning, ethical conduct, global sensitivity, and service. Those institutions that will succeed in achieving a 21st-century version of academic excellence will be those institutions that believe—in their students, in their communities, in themselves—and as a consequence of that belief, will take risks and design radically new approaches to embracing the imperative of change.

Dr. Blenda Wilson, President, California State University, Northridge,
Inaugural Address, April 30, 1993

A Self-Assessment Prior to Action

The challenges for our generation are staggering. Blenda Wilson's call to leave a legacy of harmony and opportunity for the future will require responses of a different order and quality than those we have grown used to. Everything you have learned in this workbook and more will be called upon to bail us out of the current morass and help us realize a new vision for the future.

In the earlier chapters of this book we established the essential qualities of leadership, including:

1. Knowing yourself through reflection and self-observation;
2. Understanding your history and your environment;
3. Clarifying your values and your goals;
4. Knowing and applying your learning style;
5. Being willing to be a lifelong learner;
6. Taking risks and being open to change;
7. Accepting mistakes and failure as necessary to creativity and problem solving;
8. Creating a vision and seeing yourself and your life as part of it;
9. Communicating your vision with meaning so that others are inspired by it;
10. Maintaining trust through empathy, constancy, and integrity;
11. Translating intention into reality through committed action.

In preceding chapters we have shared conceptual models, experiences and reflections of others, and numerous exercises to develop your understanding and leadership skills. The insights you gained point the way to a lifetime of learning. There is one more segment of our work together to be completed. We now address the final quality of a leader, the ability to make it happen, to realize your dreams, to translate your intention into reality, to take action and produce results.

All action is predicated on having an intention, on a person who knows what he or she wants setting out to achieve it. Some people are born knowing what they want and even how to do it. The rest of us are not so lucky. We have to spend time figuring out what to do with our lives. We are unaware of our intentions. Jamie Raskin, a former assistant attorney general of Boston, told us, "One of my heroes is a professor at Harvard Law School named Derek Bell. He told me that it's important not to have any specific ambitions or desires. It's more important to have ambitions in terms of the way you want to live your life, and then the other things will flow out of that." Derek Bell demonstrated this tenet in his own life by taking a leave of absence from Harvard Law School until the school changed its hiring practices to include African-American women.

What do you want? The majority of us go though life, often very successfully, without ever asking, much less answering, this most basic question. The first step in becoming a committed and strategic actor is to be able to answer this question. It is also to understand the relationship between your intentions and your abilities: what drives you and your satisfactions, your values, and those of the environment? Review the questions below and consider them as you prepare yourself to become a person of action.

Questions to Consider

A. What do you want? What are your abilities and capacities to have it? What is the difference between the two?

B. What drives you? What gives you satisfaction? What is the difference between the two?

C. What are your values and priorities? What are the values and priorities of your organization? What is the difference between the two?

D. Knowing the differences between what you want and what you are able to do, between what drives you and what satisfies you, and between what your values are and what your organization's values are—are you able and willing to overcome those differences?

What each of us wants is to express ourselves fully, for that is the most basic human drive. As one friend put it, "We all want to learn how to use our own voices." Effective action is based on true self-expression. As we consider the questions above, we realize that there is often a gap between what we want to achieve and our abilities, between what gives us satisfaction and what drives us, and between our values and the values of our organization. These questions allow us to conduct a self-assessment before developing our plan of action.

In the first instance, assessing our wants against our capabilities, the issues are fairly basic. Almost every one of us has, at one point in our lives, wanted to be an NFL quarterback, a movie star, a jazz singer, etc., but we simply did not have the requisite equipment. Although we have said—and believe—that you can learn anything you want to learn, certain occupations require gifts beyond learning. We know a highly successful radiologist who has always dreamed of being a singer, but has no voice. Instead of abandoning her dream, she writes songs. A would-be quarterback who is fast and smart, but weighs only 140 pounds, might well become a coach or manager, or organize a Saturday afternoon touch football league among friends and co-workers.

In the second instance, when you have to distinguish between satisfaction and drive, the issue is more complex. We all know people who are driven to succeed, never mind at what or how, who are never satisfied, and are often unhappy. It is entirely possible to succeed and satisfy yourself simultaneously, but only if you are wise enough and honest enough to admit what you want and recognize what you need.

In the third instance, when your values and those of your organization differ, we can refer back to Ed, whose case we addressed in Chapter Six. If he had thought more about what he wanted and what his company needed, he would not have driven himself off the track. But he spent his energies doing and proving, not being. Some corporate cultures are so rigid that they require absolute obedience to the corporate line. Others are flexible, adjustable, and adaptable. By knowing the degree of flex in yourself and in the organization, you will know whether you can create a fit or not.

Clarity about your goals, your sources of satisfaction, and your values is a necessary precursor to taking action. Understanding where your goals and those of your organization differ will allow you to make more informed and strategic choices.

Your Goals Statement—An Exercise

A wise proverb reminds us that if we do not know where we want to go, any road will take us there. In order to act effectively it is wise to be clear about our goals. Knowing what we want is a beginning. Having a vision is also necessary. But without clear goals that can be measured, noted, and acknowledged when achieved, we will roam around in circles. In Chapter Two when we discussed how to use this book, we asked you to create long- and short-term goals for your growth as a leader. Those goals were necessary for your effective use of yourself in this learning process. You might want to revisit them and see how they have changed as you have evolved through your work here.

This chapter represents the summation of our learning process together. In order to complete the exercises included here we would like to build on your work in previous chapters. We begin with the vision you wrote in Chapter Five. You may use the one you created for your organization, or the one that you dreamed of for your own life. Refer back to that vision. If you no longer value it or if your perspective has changed, create a new vision using the tools contained in Chapter Five.

With your vision in place, set five or six goals you would like to achieve in the next year that will bring you closer to reaching your vision. Here are the steps to use in creating goals:

Steps in Setting Goals

A. Project your image of yourself one year from now, and picture where you will be, how you will feel, what you will be doing. Try to picture what it will be like to begin to realize your vision.

B. Now create the five or six accomplishments you will have achieved at that point. Limit yourself to five or six goals. One of the dangers of too many goals is that you will become overwhelmed with all there is to do and paralyzed in a state of inaction. Fewer than five or six goals will not be comprehensive enough to make a difference.

C. These five or six accomplishments are your goals. They should be stated in the past tense, as if you have already achieved them. For example, a goal might be: "In one year our organization increased the diversity of our staff by filling all vacant positions with qualified people of color."

D. Your goals should be objectively measurable and identifiable so you can know when you have achieved them.

E. Your goals should directly support your vision and move your organization toward the vision as they are reached.

The chart below will help you create your goals. Please first refer to your vision, then create your goals in terms of your vision. You will use this chart through the rest of the exercises in this chapter.

Goal Chart (Set 5 to 6 goals to be achieved in one year to forward your vision)

1.
....

....
2.
....

....
3.
....

....
4.
....

....

5.
. . . .

. . . .

6.
. . . .

. . . .

If you are working in a team or with a partner, share your goals and ask for feedback. Ask another observer if your goals seem to support your vision. Are they achievable in one year? Do they seem worth accomplishing, worth the effort? Are there similarities to the goals of others? If so, can you see ways to support one another?

Now you know what you want, and you have your vision and goals in place; next you need to add commitment to the mix of requirements for action.

Commitment and Desire as Requisites for Action

Without commitment and desire, no action can be effective. It is not easy to bring a dream into reality. There are many stumbling blocks in the road, many mine fields laid by others, many failures waiting to discourage you. Only by having a deep and profound commitment to your vision and your goals, and by using strong desire to fuel your behavior, will you prevail. Many people we know take heart from the following statement. We often see it hanging on walls in offices and in kitchens. It speaks to commitment on all levels for all endeavors.

> Until one is committed
> there is hesitancy, the chance to draw back,
> always ineffectiveness.
> Concerning all acts of initiative (and creation),
> there is one elementary truth,
> the ignorance of which kills countless ideas
> and splendid plans:
> that the moment one definitely commits oneself,
> then Providence moves too.
> All sorts of things occur to help one
> that would never otherwise have occurred.
> A whole stream of events issues from the decision,
> raising in one's favour all manner

of unforeseen incidents and meetings
and material assistance,
which no man could have dreamt
would have come his way.

I have learned a deep respect
for one of Goethe's couplets:

"Whatever you can do, or dream you can, begin it.
Boldness has genius, power, and magic in it."
(*The Scottish Himalayan Expedition,* W. H. Murray)

The commitment Murray describes can lead to the achievement of our personal goals as well as to conquering the peaks of the Himalayas. When we speak of commitment we are talking about "stick-to-it-iveness" and perserverance. Commitment requires focus and attention. We gain a sense of purpose with commitment, and yet loss is associated with commitment. When one is committed to a course of action, a specific person, or a set of goals, we give up the alternatives. Our commitments need not be exclusive, but they call for a single-mindedness that draws us away from other choices.

Having commitments can also be embarrassing. In many organizational cultures it is the norm to be noncommittal, to hedge your bets, to play your cards close to the vest, to check out the trends and the power structure before making a move. With commitment comes revealing oneself and becoming more vulnerable. When one is committed, one acts according to one's principles and one's goals. Jamie Raskin is a leader who makes his commitments known. He points out the potential for positive results if you reveal your commitments: "If you hold your ground and make your conviction known, people will come around. I'm committed to radical principles. As Oscar Wilde said, 'I'm on the left, which is the side of the heart, as opposed to the right, which is the side of the liver.' "

Desire is a close and necessary partner to commitment. Without passion and desire, our commitments are dry and do not enliven anyone, including ourselves. Desire is a natural response, it exists in all of us. Virtually every one of us was born with a hunger for life, with what we call a passion for the promises of life. That passion can take us to the heights. Unfortunately, in too many of us, it turns into drive. Entrepreneur Larry Wilson defined the difference between desire and drive as the difference between expressing yourself and proving yourself. In a perfect world, everyone would be encouraged to express themselves and no one would be required to prove themselves, but neither the world nor we are perfect.

Learning to Lead

In order to avoid booby-trapping ourselves, we need to understand that drive is healthy only when it is married to desire.

Drive divorced from desire is always hazardous, sometimes lethal, while drive in the service of desire is always productive, and usually rewarding—in every sense of the word. Barbara Corday, CBS executive, credits her success partly to her desire expressed as enthusiasm:

> A corporation, or show, is only as strong as the caring and enthusiasm that the people who are involved in it on a daily basis put into it. And I don't think you can expect caring and enthusiasm from people you, the leader, don't care about and are not conscious of. . . . I think my enthusiasm is catching. I think when I get on a project, if I love it, I can make you love it.

Commitments and Desires—An Exercise

We now refer back to the vision and goals you created and work to realize them. Revealed in your vision and goals are your commitments and passions in life. In this exercise we ask you to use self-reflection you developed in your previous work. We would like you to analyze your vision and your goals, and reveal your commitments and desires. For example, in doing this exercise, if you had the goal of increasing the diversity of your organization by making sure that each vacated position was filled by a qualified person of color, you would acknowledge that you are committed to diversity in the work environment; to enabling people of color to have the same opportunities as Caucasians; and to making up for past discrimination with remedial action to balance the staff in your organization.

Often we are not conscious of our commitments until they are uncovered in our behavior or until they are challenged by someone else. How many romances turn on the impending loss of a loved one, and only then is commitment revealed? How many social change movements are built as individuals become committed through participating or through experiencing the problem directly? Often we are unaware of what we care about until we act, until in the process of acting, we discover our passions. When we are unconscious of our convictions, we are unable to be strategic or win others to our side. In the following exercise we ask you to become aware of your convictions and to explore their origins so you can claim them and use them more powerfully to guide your behavior and enlist the support of others.

150

Steps in Revealing Commitments

A. Review your vision and goals statement. In the space provided below, list as many commitments as you can identify that are embedded in your vision and goals. Do not censor any ideas. This is a personal brainstorming process. Even if some commitments seem outlandish or extreme, write every one of them down.

....

....

....

....

....

....

....

....

....

....

B. Now review your list. Were you surprised by any commitments on you list? Which ones are your true commitments? Which ones would you stand or fall behind? Where is your passion with regard to these commitments?

C. Create a chart of your true commitments, those you feel passionately about. Use the chart on page 152. Notice which ones were unconscious before this exercise. Which commitments did you discover? Which ones were conscious and which were unconscious? Is there a pattern you can discern?

D. Which commitments do you usually express openly? Which ones are more private? How does your family, your organization, and your social circle support or block expression of your commitments? Are there any commitments about which you feel passionately and want to express more consistently in your life?

E. Which ones are obviously part of your identity? Share your list with someone who knows you well. Would they be able to guess your commitments? Discuss their perceptions of your commitments and learn more about how others see you.

F. On your chart of commitments there is a space next to each one. In this space indicate the origin of this commitment. Is it something you learned in your family or from a mentor or friend? Is so, indicate who taught it to you and how they expressed it. Is it something you created out of your experience? If so, describe the experience in which you developed or adopted this commitment. What do you notice about the origin of your commitments?

G. If you are working with a group, share your commitments and their origins. Notice the different commitments and how they are expressed by each of you. Discuss how each of you can be supported to more openly express and live by your commitments. Discuss how you can bring your passion into the work environment more successfully.

Commitments Chart

TRUE COMMITMENTS	ORIGIN
....	....
....	....
....	....
....	....
....	....
....	....
....	....
....	....
....	....

Commitments and passions belong to the heart. Leaders must also work from the mind to create effective action. Strategic thinking is a key skill for leadership. Without a strategy to guide action, we are reduced to trial and error with no overall plan.

Strategic Thinking

There is an old saying: "Unless you are the lead dog, the scenery never changes." To extend that thought: For the leader, the scenery is always changing, everything is new. Because, by definition, each leader is unique, the circumstances are perceived uniquely. Out of the leader's role in dealing with the chaos of our times and the constancy of change comes the demand that leaders be strategic thinkers. A well-developed strategy allows leaders to think of solutions to problems that may not have manifested yet. A strategy takes the leader out of the reaction mode and provides for creativity and initiative. The capacity for strategic thinking is one of the intangible traits of leadership that is difficult to teach.

Sydney Pollack, when asked if leadership could be taught, responded, "It's hard to teach anything that can't be broken down into repeatable and unchanging elements. Driving a car, flying an airplane—you can reduce those things to a series of maneuvers that are always executed in the same way. But with something like leadership, just as with art, you reinvent the wheel every single time you apply the principle." Robert Dockson agreed: "Leaders aren't technicians."

Creativity and strategy are interconnected then, for bankers as well as motion-picture directors. The creative process that underlies strategic thinking is infinitely complex, yet there are basic steps in the process that can be identified. When you reduce something to its most elemental state, its nuclear core, you can generalize from there.

First, whether you are planning a novel or a corporate reorganization, you need to know where you begin and where you want to end up. Mountain climbers start climbing from the bottom of the mountain, but they look at where they want to go and work backward to their starting point. Like a mountain climber, once you have the summit in view, you can figure out all the ways you might get there. Then you play with those choices—altering, connecting, compromising, revising, and imaging—finally choosing one or two routes.

Second, you flesh out those routes, elaborate them, revise them, and map them, complete with possible pitfalls and traps as well as rewards.

Third, you look to see if the direct route is the most sound, or whether you should make a more circuitous approach.

Fourth, you plan your resources and identify your allies.

Learning to Lead

Fifth, you examine your map objectively, as if you were not its maker. You locate all its soft spots, and eliminate them or change them.

Finally, when you have finished the strategy, you set out to climb the mountain.

Frances Hesselbein together with her husband and their families have been a part of Johnstown, Pennsylvania, for four generations. They had a communications business and she worked as a Girl Scout volunteer there, but also did management training for Girl Scout councils around the country. Asked to take over the CEO slot of the local council temporarily, she agreed. Six years later, though she had not applied for the job, she was made executive director of the Girl Scouts of USA. She and her husband moved to New York City and set about reorganizing the Scouts, to reflect everything she had learned on her way up the ladder. She describes her experiences this way:

> The first thing we did . . . was to develop a corporate planning system in which planning and management were synonymous. It was a common planning system for 335 local councils and the national organization. We developed a corporate planning monograph to mobilize the energy of 600,000 adult volunteers in order to carry out our mission to help young girls grow up and reach their highest potential as women. Today, our people feel we've achieved more unity and cohesion than anyone can remember.

> I just felt there was compelling need to . . . have a clear planning system that defined roles, differentiating between the volunteers, and the operational staff, and the policy planners, one that permitted whatever was going on in the smallest troop—needs, trends, whatever—to flow through to the policy makers, so they had a clear idea of what was going on and what needed to go on. We have three million members, and we really listen to the girls and their parents, and we've devised ways to reach out to the girls wherever they are. We say, "We have something of value to offer you, but you in return have something to offer us. We respect your values and culture, and if you open our handbooks, even if you are a minority, a Navajo, you're there." The best thing about it is that every girl in America can look at the program and see herself.

Hesselbein had a vision of a responsive, inclusive organization. Her strategy was to use a planning system to move the Girl Scouts in that direction, and she was successful.

154

There are risks in making the results of your strategic thinking real. But as author Carlos Casteneda said, "The basic difference between an ordinary man and a warrior is that a warrior takes everything as a challenge, while an ordinary man takes everything as a blessing or a curse." This is the challenge of leadership, to see a vision and bring it to fruition.

The Strategy Map—An Exercise

The concept of strategy originated in the military. It grew out of the need to achieve a position through the movement of troops, supplies, and ammunition so as not to alert the enemy in order to defeat them. Using strategy in an organization need not involve conflict or defeat to achieve one's goals. Strategies are, however, driven by a need to achieve something that is desired. They take into consideration many variables, including human relations, politics, and social factors as well as costs, materials, and logistics. You need not apply a command-and-control style to implement a strategy. The leaders we admire are able to include others in creating their strategy and carrying it out. The most successful strategic leaders behave as Lao Tzu describes:

> Fail to honor people,
> They fail to honor you;
> But of a good leader, who talks little,
> When his work is done, his aim fulfilled,
> They will all say, "We did this ourselves."

In the exercise below you will create a strategy map. To do this, you will need to select a goal from those you identified earlier. As an example, we chose the goal of increasing diversity in our organization by filling all vacant positions this year with qualified people of color. Pick a goal that you would like to reach in actuality and write it below:

A. A goal for which you would like to create a strategy:

. . . .

. . . .

. . . .

In order to create a strategy map, you will need to think of your goal as a destination. It is somewhere you would like to go to. You also need to identify a starting point. For example, in working with our goal, our starting point is that 1 percent of our staff are people of color. Also, the personnel department is resistant to our goal and therefore not enthusiastic about recruiting suitable candidates. In addition, we do not know how many positions will be available this year, so we cannot monitor the openings and the hiring process. Finally, we are unaware of the talent pool available to fill these positions. To create your strategy you must analyze your starting point as we did so you know where you are beginning from and where you are going to end up. Where you will end up is your goal.

B. Fill in your starting point, from which you will mount your strategy:

....

....

....

....

....

....

....

....

In order to begin your strategy map you must have a clear assessment of the allies you can count on and the resources at your disposal. For example, in our case we would have to know who in the personnel department might be more receptive to achieving our goal. We might have to do a cost analysis of the plan to identify the resources we have, and will need to support the recruitment effort. We might also identify other organizations that have achieved similar goals and recruit allies from these programs. For your strategy to be successful, you must know your allies, the resources you have at your disposal, and those that are needed.

C. List your allies, the resources you have and those that are needed:

....

....

....

....

....

....

Now you are ready to create your strategy map. The map is a visual representation of your strategy. Strategies are high-level tools. They are not specific action, tactics, or behaviors. They give you a fall-back position to which you can always return if a particular action is not successful. Too often when we fail we give up on our goal completely. If you have a strategy and a particular tactic fails, you can return to the strategy and regroup.

For example, our strategy to reach our goal might be to involve the personnel department so that they embrace our goal as theirs and are committed to achieving it in partnership with us. If this is our strategy and the first meeting we have with them bombs, we need not give up. Our strategy is not to have a meeting with them, our strategy is to get them involved. So we can analyze the meeting, learn from our mistakes, and try another tactic. This might be meeting individually with each person to identify our natural allies before going back to the department as a whole. Our strategy keeps us on course and focused on our goal at all times.

Using the Strategy Map model on page 158, create a strategy map for achieving your goal. In the lower left-hand corner note your starting point, and in the upper right-hand corner put your goal. Map A shows one straightforward example. Connect the starting point and the goal with a line. If your strategy is direct the line will be straight, connecting the two points by the shortest route, as shown in Map A. If you must take a more circuitous route, your strategy will look like Map B.

Now include your allies and the resources you have or will need. You may show these supportive elements to your strategy as indicated on Maps A and B. Place your allies above the line and your resources below. This picture will give you a clear idea of your strategy and how you can support it.

If you are working with others you may want to draw your maps on a large piece of flip-chart paper or on a white board. Otherwise, you can use the strategy map worksheet provided on page 158. Share your strategies with your colleagues and reality check with them. Do your colleagues agree with your analysis of allies and resources? Have you created the

Strategy Map

GOAL:

ALLIES:

RESOURCES:

STRATEGY:

STARTING POINT:

Map A

GOAL:
Positions Filled with
People of Color

ALLIES:

Other Organizations with Experience

Executive Managers who
Support the Goal

Line Managers Who Want
to Hire People of Color

Individuals in Personnel
Who Support the Goal

STRATEGY:
Have the Personnel Department Own the Goal and Commit to Achieving It

RESOURCES:

Travel Money for Candidates
for Positions

Funds for Special Recruitment

Recruiters and Head Hunters
with Good Contacts

Funds for Special Meetings
to Create Buy-in for Goal

STARTING POINT:
1 Percent of Staff Are
People of Color

Map B

GOAL:
Positions Filled with
People of Color

ALLIES:

Individuals in Personnel
Who Support the Goal

Other Organizations
with Experience

Line Managers and
Executives Who Support
the Goal

Trainers Who Can
Do Workshops

Have Personnel Own the
Goal and Commit To It

RESOURCES:
Funds for Recruitment,
Advertising, etc.

Travel Money for
Candidates

Funds for Speakers and
Educational Programs

Funds for Special Meetings
for Education

Create Awareness
of Problem

Build Concern
in Organization

STARTING POINT:
1 Percent of Staff Are People
of Color

most powerful strategy? What are the pitfalls and dangers faced by your strategy? Can they support yours? Will you support theirs?

Power to Achieve Your Goals—Exercises

No discussion of translating visions into reality would be complete without reference to power. We often associate power with force, but it is a more complex dynamic than it appears. With coercive power there is usually a tangible reward for compliance. It is a simple transaction that is based on a material relationship. Another type of power comes from identification with the source of power. Recipients emulate the person with whom they identify and carry out her or his bidding. A third type of power comes with expertise. The person on the receiving end attains the knowledge of the expert. There is also group power that is normative. The members of the group respond to the power of the whole by following the norms of the culture. There is power of access, in which people, goods, and decision-making authority become available through contacts. There is the power of persuasion, in which the recipient is won over to a side or a point through an argument or convincing demonstration. Finally, there is the power of empowering others, in which the recipient experiences respect, support, and growth.

Each type of power can be useful depending on the goal, starting point, and strategy you are employing. For example, if we are mounting the strategy mapped above in which we want the personnel department to be responsible for our goal, it would not be useful to employ a coercive form of power. Rather, we would use an empowering approach. However, if we were conducting a training program on diversity, we would use our expertise and hope the participants would gain knowledge. We would also encourage them to emulate us through the power of identification.

Kareem Abdul Jabar, the Los Angles Laker star forward for many years, writes of the empowering leadership we envision in his autobiography. He ascribes this leadership to his UCLA coach, John Wooden, who gave him his start and empowered him in his early years:

> As a competitor, he was unnerving. Many coaches in the then Pac 8 didn't like him because he was too good to be believed. He wanted to win, but not more than anything. Coach Wooden wanted to win very much, but within the rules, within the guidelines he had set for the expression of his own and his players' competitive talent. Within those, he went all out. He understood the game totally. He eliminated the possibility of defeat. It was genius. . . . I don't know why fate placed me in his hands, but I'm

grateful that it did. My relationship with him has been one of the most significant of my life. He believed in what he was doing and what we were doing together. He had faith in us as players and as people. He was about winning basketball and winning as human beings. The consummate teacher, he taught us that doing the best you are capable of is victory enough, and that you can't walk until you can crawl, that gentle but profound truth about growing up. . . .

How have you expressed and used power in your own life? Your history with power, as it was practiced toward you and as you have used it, will affect your use of power as a leader. In this exercise, you will explore experiences in which you have used different types of power to achieve a goal. This is an opportunity to discover the type of power you have used and the limits or opportunities it provided. Again, this activity of self-reflection will allow you to become conscious of your use of power and enable you to choose the form of power you will use as a leader.

On the chart we have listed the types of power we distinguished above. Remember a time when you used this type of power effectively to achieve a particular result. Describe the incident briefly, then reflect on the limits and opportunities provided by the use of that form of power.

TYPE OF POWER	INCIDENT	LIMITS	OPPORTUNITIES
Coercive			
Identification			
Expert			

Group
....

....

....

Access
....

....

....

Persuasion
....

....

....

Empowerment
....

....

....

When you have completed your chart, share it with your colleagues. Did they find one form of power more limiting than others? Did you have similar examples of the use of power from your organization? What expressions of power are reinforced in your organization? What would have to change for empowerment to be the form of power most frequently employed?

As you reflect on your own experience, think about how comfortable you feel with each form of power. What would it take for you to use empowerment to achieve your goal? As you ready yourself to make your vision a reality, consider empowerment as your expression of power.

Write a scenario below in which you would use empowerment to realize your goal. You may have to reconsider your strategy to incorporate a more inclusive and empowering approach. Include how you will enact your strategy, who will be involved, how will you empower them, what their behaviors will look like, and what results you will achieve.

Learning to Lead

Achieving Your Goal through Empowerment:

. . . .

. . . .

. . . .

. . . .

. . . .

. . . .

. . . .

. . . .

. . . .

. . . .

. . . .

. . . .

. . . .

. . . .

. . . .

. . . .

. . . .

. . . .

. . . .

Empowerment: A Conclusion

Empowerment is at the heart of all our work in this workbook; it is the collective effect of leadership. In organizations with effective leaders, empowerment is most evident in four themes or feelings. When these themes exist, organizations are successful and leaders are fulfilled. We offer these themes as a final benediction to you as you complete this course in leadership and begin your journey as a lifelong leader.

In an organization in which leaders lead through empowerment:

> **People feel significant.** Everyone in the organization, at least in some way, feels he or she makes a difference to the success of the organization. Whether it is delivering potato chips to a small mom-and-pop store in western Colorado or developing a small but essential part for an airplane, where there is empowerment, people feel their work is connected to the world, that what they do has meaning and significance.

> **Learning and competence matter.** Leaders value learning and mastery. Leon Fleischer turned down Warren Bennis's offer to be Dean of the School of Music at the University of Cincinnati because he wanted to stay with his orthopedic therapy, to learn what he needed to learn to regain the use of his hand. As most people know, he succeeded and returned to the concert stage. So leaders value learning and so do the people who work for leaders. Leaders make it clear that there is no failure—only mistakes that give us feedback and tell us what to do next.

> **People are part of a community.** Where there is leadership, there is a team, a family, unity. Even people who do not especially like each other feel the sense of community. When Neil Armstrong, the first man on the moon, talks about the Apollo explorations, he tells us how an almost unimaginably complex set of interdependent tasks were carried out by a team. The team worked beautifully. It felt like a loving family.

> **Work is exciting.** Where there are leaders who empower, the work is stimulating, challenging, fascinating, and fun. An essential ingredient in organizational leadership is that the leader pulls rather than pushes people along. A pull style of influence works by attracting and energizing people to enroll in their vision of the future. It motivates through identification rather than through rewards and punishments. The leader in such an organization articulates and if possible, embodies the ideals toward which the organization strives. Members of the organization enroll themselves in a vision that is attainable, and their behavior exemplifies the ideal in action.

Learning to Lead

It is also apparent that organization members cannot be expected to enroll in any kind of vision. Some visions and concepts have more staying power and are more deeply rooted in our human hungers than others. We believe that the lack of two concepts in modern organizational life is in large part responsible for the alienation and lack of meaning that so many managers and workers experience in their work.

One of these concepts is the idea of *quality*. Modern industrial society has been oriented to *quantity*, to providing more goods and services for everyone. In this preoccupation, we have inevitably failed to keep quality in the forefront. Quantity is measured in money; we have become a money-oriented society. Quality is often not measured at all, but is appreciated intuitively. Our response to quality is a feeling: Feelings of quality are intimately connected with our experience of meaning and beauty and values in our lives.

Closely linked to the concept of quality is that of *dedication,* even love, of quality and organization. This dedication is evoked by quality and is the attracting force that energizes high-performance systems. When we love our work, when it has quality, we do not have to be managed by hopes of rewards or fears of punishment. We can create systems that facilitate our work rather than being preoccupied with checks and controls of people who want to beat or exploit the system.

We hope you will continue to develop what you have begun in the learning partnership we created here together. We look forward to knowing you more directly in the future.

Empowerment leads to quality and ultimately to love of ourselves, of our work, and of life. More we cannot wish you.

Books on Leadership
An Annotated Bibliography

Anthony Khoo
Hyepin Im

This bibliography was compiled from a survey of top-level managers and academicians in the field of leadership research. They were asked to provide their choices for the top five leadership books.

The top books are presented here, with the author's name in alphabetical order. A short description for each book is included to provide a brief understanding of what the book has to offer and how the author presents the material.

The Art of Japanese Management
Anthony Athos and Richard Pascale, Warner Books, 1982

> The authors examine, in depth, the philosophy and operations of Japan's Matsushita Electric Company and compare them with a similar American corporation, ITT. Pascale and Athos conclude that successful management is based on Seven S's: strategy, structure, systems, staff, style, skills, and superordinate goals. They maintain

167

that the fundamental differences between U.S. companies and their Japanese competitors lie not in organizational structures or systems but in areas related to managerial style and cultivated skills.

Leadership and the Quest for Integrity
Joseph L. Badaracco and Richard R. Ellsworth, Harvard Business School Press, 1989

The authors argue that the ability to change style to fit the situation is not a positive attribute for leaders. Instead, integrity and a daily quest for consistency of personal beliefs, and creating a vision for the organization, are the surest paths to leadership.

Bass and Stogdill's Handbook of Leadership
Bernard Bass, Free Press, 1990

This book consists of thirty-seven chapters and is divided into eight parts. It is not the sort of work you will sit down and read from cover to cover. However, it is more than just an encyclopedia of research findings, and the reader will certainly benefit from tackling a chapter, or even a group of chapters, all at once for the sake of comprehension and continuity.

Organizing Genius: The Secrets of Creative Collaboration
Warren Bennis and Patricia Ward Biederman, Addison-Wesley, 1997

Moving beyond the "Great Man" model of leadership, Bennis and Biederman present the notion of "Great Groups," synergistic collaborations that have left an enduring legacy. The authors examine Walt Disney Studios, Xerox Palo Alto Research Center, Apple Computer, the 1992 Clinton campaign, Lockheed's Skunk Works, Black Mountain College, and the Manhattan Project. From these stories, important lessons emerge. The Great Group and its great leader create each other. A Great Group starts with superb people; has a strong leader; is composed of talented people *who can work together;* thinks it is a mission from God; is an island, with its own culture; sees itself as a winning underdog; always has an enemy, real or invented; has tunnel vision, seeing only the project; is optimistic rather than realistic; allows its members to find their own place on the project; and completes its task. A Great Group leader loves talent and knows where to find it, gives the group what it needs, and shields the group from petty distractions. Finally, in a Great Group, great work is its own reward.

Leaders: The Strategies for Taking Charge (Second Edition)
Warren Bennis and Burt Nanus, Harper Business, 1997
> This work is the outcome of 90 interviews of business (60) and public-sector (30) leaders. The authors found two common attributes: 1) that leaders gave vision to their organizations, and 2) that leaders had the ability to translate those visions into reality.

On Becoming a Leader (Second Edition)
Warren Bennis, Addison-Wesley, 1994
> The first edition of this work was the fruit of personal interviews with sixty business leaders and thirty public-sector leaders. Two essential components of leadership emerged in these interviews: creating a vision, and translating that vision into reality. The second edition contains updated examples and elaborates upon the original analysis by emphasizing the following six principles: 1) Leadership is about character. 2) To keep organizations competitive, leaders must help to create a social architecture capable of generating intellectual capital. 3) Realizing a vision requires conviction and passion. 4) A leader must generate and sustain trust. 5) True leaders enroll others in their vision through optimism. 6) Leaders have a bias toward action that results in success.

Why Leaders Can't Lead: The Unconscious Conspiracy Continues
Warren Bennis, Jossey-Bass, 1989
> Bennis attributes the obstacles facing leaders to an unconscious conspiracy in contemporary society, which prevents leaders from taking charge and making changes. The author offers new insights and a more clearly developed conceptualization of the failures of present-day institutional leadership based on his and others' observations during the last several decades.

Leadership
James MacGregor Burns, Harper & Row, 1979
> Leadership is organized into 5 sections: 1) a general introduction and guidelines; 2) examining the origins of leadership using examples such as Gandhi and Wilson; 3) transforming leadership which is leadership that shapes and alters and elevates the motives and values and goals of followers; 4) transactional leadership, which is defined as a reciprocal process of mobilizing various resources to realize goals held by both leaders and followers; and 5) implications: theory and practice.

Bibliography

Thank God It's Monday! 14 Values We Need to Humanize the Way We Work
Kenneth Cloke and Joan Goldsmith, Irwin Professional Publishing, 1997

> *Thank God It's Monday!* spotlights the often-neglected human component of the change process, and calls for a more humane and fulfilling work environment. The 14 values, which are illustrated with real-life examples, are Inclusion, Collaboration, Teams & Networks, Vision, Celebration of Diversity, Process Awareness, Open and Honest Communication, Risk Taking, Paradoxical Problem Solving, Individual and Team Ownership of Results, Everyone Is a Leader, Personal Growth & Satisfaction, Conflict as Opportunity, and Embracing Change. The focus is on effecting practical organizational change; the authors offer nineteen exercises designed to assist the manager in integrating these fourteen values into the workplace.

Leadership Is an Art
Max DePree, Doubleday, 1989

> The author calls this book a book of ideas that demands something of you and on which you can continually build. The overall philosophy is summed up thus: "The first responsibility of a leader is to define reality. The last is to say thank you. In between the two, the leader must become a servant and a debtor."

Leading Minds: An Anatomy of Leadership
Howard Gardner, with Emma Laskin, Basic Books, 1995

> Gardner creates a cognitive framework for all that has been learned about leadership. Effective leaders have four characteristics. These are: a tie to a community or audience, a rhythm of life that includes isolation and immersion, a relationship between the stories they tell and the traits they embody, and arrival at power through the choice of the people rather than by brute force. The author fleshes out his theory with minibiographies of eleven twentieth-century leaders, beginning with Margaret Mead and ending with Mahatma Gandhi.

On Leadership
John W. Gardner, Free Press, 1989

> The author presents a lucid, readable analysis of the varied and often complex characteristics of leadership. Gardner analyzes such aspects as power, motivation, commitment, leaders and followers, shared values, and institution renewal. He says that we should not confuse leadership with status. Leaders always have some power, but it is possible to have power and not be a leader.

The Tao of Leadership: Lao Tzu's Tao Te Ching *Adapted for a New Age*
John Heider, Humanics/New Age, 1985

> Heider, a Gestalt psychologist, has reworked the Tao, a great but difficult piece of work, into a manual for today's leaders. In this book, he tries not to shift the meaning or the emphasis of several of the poems in order to make the implicit explicit, and to be prescriptive.

Leadership Without Easy Answers
Ronald A. Heifetz, Harvard University Press, 1994

> These thoughtful, literate reflections on leadership are intended for leaders as well as those who look to them for answers. Heifetz's model of leadership is a social contract where constituents confer power and resources in return for leadership and guidance. The social contract between leader and follower requires insight and sensitivity on the part of the leader, and realistic expectations on the part of the follower. The transformation of a dominance relationship into more mutually participative social contract is no small event—it is a revolution. The five strategic principles of leadership are: 1) Identify the adaptive challenge. 2) Keep the level of distress within a tolerable range. 3) Focus attention on ripening issues. 4) Give the work back to people, but at a rate they can stand. 5) Protect voices of dissent.

The Change Masters: Innovation for Productivity in the American Mode
Rosabeth Moss Kanter, Simon & Schuster, 1983

> Kanter defines change masters as "those people and organizations adept at the art of anticipating the need for, and of leading, productive change." Part of the reason America is in trouble is the "quiet suffocation of the entrepreneurial spirit in segmentalist companies." Interviews and case studies form the foundation for this argument in support of innovation and change.

A Force for Change
John P. Kotter, Free Press, 1990

> In this book the author combines questionnaires and detailed case studies to yield fresh insights into how corporations really work—and how they don't. Kotter also provides a schematic to illustrate the difference between leadership and management. The author feels that managers execute by monitoring results against the plans, and leaders execute by motivating and inspiring people to overcome bureaucratic hurdles.

Bibliography

The Leadership Factor
John P. Kotter, Free Press, 1988

> Kotter discusses what he sees as "the need for leadership" at all levels of management and aims to describe the kind required for the United States to remain competitive. He considers how business is changing and the impact of these changes on leadership, makes recommendations, and discusses how to implement the recommendations.

The Leadership Challenge: How to Get Extraordinary Things Done in Organizations
James M. Kouzes and Barry Z. Posner, Jossey-Bass, 1987

> This book on leadership for business executives covers such topics as identifying and developing leadership qualities and building commitment into action. The authors do not simply recount the experiences of some of the 500 managers they interview, but use them to build and illustrate a model of leadership.

Corporate Pathfinders: Building Vision and Values into Organizations
Harold J. Leavitt, Dow Jones-Irwin, 1986

> Leavitt's new model of the management process involves three steps: pathfinding (getting the right questions rather than the right answers); problem solving (analysis—reason and logic); and implementing (action). He further defines pathfinding as the "number one" management thrust, but concludes that pathfinding is difficult to exercise in a sluggish organization; he envisions the possibility of a pathfinding culture.

The Connective Edge: Leading in an Interdependent World
Jean Lipman-Blumen, Jossey-Bass, 1996

> In an age of increasing global interdependence, the "connective" leader is the one who will be successful. Lipman-Blumen describes nine leadership styles that fall into three main categories:
> Relational: Mentors, Helps, Collaborates
> Instrumental: Empowers, Networks, Persuades
> Direct: Takes charge, Outperforms, Excels
> Connective leaders can move among these styles as the situation requires, achieving "flexibility through behavioral option." The connective leader has a superior feel for interdependence and an eye for diversity. A section on women leaders explores the complex question of whether gender makes a difference in leadership. The idea that women naturally and universally employ connective leadership is not borne out in real life. Leaders of both sexes must work at cultivating connective leadership.

Bibliography

The Prince
Niccolo Machiavelli, 1532

> A new translation, with an introduction by Harvey C. Mansfield, University of Chicago Press, 1985

> Mansfield's work is the most recent of a spate of new translations of Machiavelli's classic, and it is worth acquiring as the best combination of accuracy and readability. Many translations do not respect carefully enough Machiavelli's use of special terms (e.g. *virtu*), but Mansfield tries to leave English readers with the raw materials from which to construct their own interpretation. Mansfield also includes brief useful notes on persons or events that Machiavelli describes.

The Leader's Edge
Burt Nanus, Contemporary Books, 1989

> In this book, the author tells us that leadership has been too preoccupied with 1) the present at the expense of the future, and 2) the internal environment at the expense of the external one. Nanus also describes the seven interrelated "megaskills" that he feels are required: farsightedness, mastery of interdependence, anticipatory learning, high standards of integrity, mastery of change, initiative, and organization design.

Leading Change: Overcoming the Ideology of Comfort and the Tyranny of Custom
James O'Toole, Jossey-Bass, 1995

> O'Toole uses painter James Ensor's *Christ's Entry into Brussels in 1889* as a springboard to this work on value-based leadership. Ensor's provocative painting depicts the Redeemer engulfed in the midst of a crowd, rather than out front leading the crowd. O'Toole uses this to illustrate the challenge of leadership today. The modern world offers many distractions, and the modern individual may be disinclined to follow anyone. "Contingency leadership," which requires leaders to adapt to circumstances, is expedient but ultimately ineffective. Only value-based leadership is powerful enough to break through the inertia of comfort and custom.

Managing on the Edge: How the Smartest Companies Use Conflict to Stay Ahead
Richard T. Pascale, Simon & Schuster, 1990

> Pascale suggests that to avoid stagnation and to be renewed, an organization should operate on the principles of fit, split, contend, and transcend. He argues that instead of searching for stability, modern management must embrace disequilibrium and transcend the old focus on control and reduction of ambiguity.

Bibliography

Leading People: Transforming Business from the Inside Out
Robert Rosen with Paul B. Brown, Viking, 1996

> The book is divided into eight sections corresponding to eight principles of leadership: vision, trust, participation, learning, diversity, creating, integrity, and community. These principles are illustrated with profiles of thirty-six of America's current notable leaders. Although leading people is hard work, leaders who honor their followers' humanity will be rewarded with success. The best, most effective leaders pay at least as much attention to principles and people as they do to profits, and the healthy enterprises that these leaders build tend to perform very well.

Organizational Culture and Leadership (Second Edition)
Edgar H. Schein, Jossey-Bass, 1992

> The author describes the concept of organizational culture and how it develops. Leaders and founders embed, transmit, and employ culture and subculture to fulfill organizational goals. Understanding culture is crucial because it enables leaders to introduce new technologies to the organization and to manage across cultural and ethnic boundaries. The essence of culture lies in shared assumptions. In order to manage culture, a leader must decipher these assumptions. Schein recommends enrolling the entire group in the task of deciphering and interpreting its own culture. This process carries risks: The analysis may be incorrect, and the organization may not be ready to receive feedback about its culture. Ultimately, the leader must foster a "learning organization," which contains the cultural mechanisms to manage and diagnose itself.

The Fifth Discipline: The Art and Practice of the Learning Organization
Peter M. Senge, Doubleday/Currency, 1990

> The author proposes the "systems thinking" method to help a corporation to become a "learning organization," one that integrates at all personnel levels in differently related company functions (sales product design, etc.) to "expand the ability to produce." Other disciplines described include "personal mastery" of one's capacities and "team learning" through group discussion of individual objectives and problems.

Certain Trumpets: The Nature of Leadership
Garry Wills, Simon and Schuster, 1995

> Wills presents leadership as a mutually determined exchange between leader and follower: "To sound a certain trumpet does not mean just trumpeting one's own certitudes. It means sounding a specific call to specific people capable of response."

Leadership can only come into being with a combination of the right followers, the right goal, and the right historical circumstances. Thus, not everyone is meant to be a leader. Wills's concept of serendipitous leadership is illustrated with sixteen biographies, each illustrating leadership in a particular context. These sixteen examples include Electoral: Franklin Roosevelt, Charismatic: King David, and Saintly: Dorothy Day. These biographies are extensively footnoted and documented.

The Leader's Companion: Insights on Leadership Through the Ages
J. Thomas Wren, The Free Press, 1995

Wren presents a comprehensive collection of writings on leadership by a wide variety of experts and philosophers. Contemporary contributors include respected academics such as James MacGregor Burns and Bernard Bass. Wren also offers classic selections from Tolstoy, Plato, Aristotle, Machiavelli, and Lao-tzu. The book is divided into thirteen topics: The Crisis of Leadership, What Is Leadership?, Historical Views of Leadership, Modern Views of Leadership, The Leader, The Followers, Leaders and Followers Together, The Leadership Environment, Leading Individuals, Leading Groups, The Skills of a Leader, Leadership in Practice, and Practicing Moral Leadership. Wren provides a brief preface to each of the thirteen sections, building a framework for the readings that follow.

Leadership in Organizations
Gary A. Yukl, Prentice-Hall, Inc., 1981

This book has ten chapters and covers topics that include power and leader effectiveness, role, expectancy and adaptive-reactive theories, and determinants of effective group decisions. The author also deals with situational aspects of leadership and effectiveness behavior, and provides a summary of participation research. Although this book provides little additional integration of the perplexing and controversial leadership issues for the veteran reader, it does render a clear summary of basic issues for the new student of leadership.

References

Chapter 1

2 Robert H. Waterman, *Adhocracy: The Power to Change,* W. W. Norton, New York, 1992.

3 Sidney Rittenberg, personal communication with Joan Goldsmith, August 14, 1993.

7 Harlan Cleveland, *The Knowledge Executive,* E. P. Dutton, New York, 1985.

8 John W. Gardner, *On Leadership,* The Free Press, New York, 1990.

Chapter 2

23 Germain Greer, *The Change,* Alfred A. Knopf, New York, 1992.

25 Norman Lear, in Warren Bennis, *On Becoming a Leader,* Addison-Wesley, Reading, Mass., 1989.

Chapter 3

60 *Franz Kafka Diaries,* ed. Max Brod. Schocken Books, New York, 1948–49.

63 Susan Griffin, *A Chorus of Stones,* Doubleday, New York, 1992.

Chapter 4

70 Max DePree, *Leadership Jazz,* Doubleday, New York, 1992.

83 John Cleese, "No More Mistakes and You're Through," *Forbes,* May 16, 1988.

References

87 David Hare, *New York Times*, Sunday, November 10, 1991.

92 John Sculley, "Sculley's Lessons from Inside Apple," *Fortune*, September 14, 1987.

95 Arnold Hiatt, "Building Corporate Character: An Interview with Stride Rite Chairman Arnold Hiatt," *Harvard Business Review*, March–April, 1992.

95 Will Schultz, *The Human Element*, in press, Jossey Bass.

Chapter 5

100 Max DePree, *Leadership Is an Art*, University of Michigan Press, East Lansing, Michigan, 1988.

101 George Bernard Shaw, *Man and Superman*, Penguin Books, Baltimore, 1973.

101 Lincoln Kirstein, in Warren Bennis and Burt Nanus, *Leaders: The Strategies for Taking Charge*, Harper & Row, New York, 1985, pages 30–1.

102 Barbara Corday, in Warren Bennis, *On Becoming a Leader*, Addison-Wesley, Reading, Mass., 1989, page 156.

103 Don Ritchey, in Warren Bennis, *On Becoming a Leader*, Addison-Wesley, Reading, Mass., 1989, page 157.

103 Frank Dale, in Warren Bennis and Burt Nanus, *Leaders: The Strategies for Taking Charge*, Harper & Row, New York, 1985.

105 John Sculley, "Sculley's Lessons from Inside Apple," *Fortune*, September 14, 1987.

111 Arlene Blum, *Annapurna, A Woman's Place*, Sierra Club Books, San Francisco, 1980.

112 Beth Jandernoa, From *The Leadership and Mastery Course* by Innovation Associates, Beth Jandernoa and Alain Gauthier, Innovation Associates, Framingham, Mass.

116 Senator John Tunney, quoted in *New York Times*, June 7, 1989.

118 Marshall Frady, "Profiles: Jesse Jackson, Part II," *New Yorker*, February 10, 1992.

Chapter 6

124 Sydney Pollack, in Warren Bennis, *On Becoming a Leader*, Addison-Wesley, Reading, Mass., 1989.

125 Norman Paul, "Parental Empathy" in *Parenthood*, E. James Anthony and Therese Benedek, eds., Little, Brown, New York, 1970.

132 Boris Pasternak, *Doctor Zhivago*, Pantheon, 1958.

"Whatever Happened to Ethics?" *Time*, May 25, 1987.

134 Harold Williams, in Warren Bennis and Burt Nanus, *Leaders: The Strategies for Taking Charge*, Harper & Row, New York, 1985.

134 Thomas L. Friedman, *New York Times*, Sunday, February 14, 1993.

135 John Gardner, "The Antileadership Vaccine" in *No Easy Victories*, Annual Report of the Carnegie Corporation, New York, 1965.

136 Aristotle, *The Ethics of Aristotle*, J.A.K. Thomson, trans., Penguin Books, New York, 1976.

142 *A Testament of Hope: The Essential Writing of Martin Luther King, Jr.*, ed. James Melvin Washington. Harper & Row, San Francisco, 1986.

Chapter 7

144 Jamie Raskin, in Warren Bennis, *On Becoming a Leader*, Addison-Wesley, Reading, Mass., 1989, page 123.

148 W. H. Murray, *The Scottish Himalayan Expedition*, J.M. Dent & Sons Ltd., London, 1951.

150 Barbara Corday, in Warren Bennis, *On Becoming a Leader*, Addison-Wesley, Reading, Mass., 1989, page 130.

153 Sydney Pollack and Robert Dockson, in Warren Bennis, *On Becoming a Leader*, Addison-Wesley, Reading, Mass., 1989, page 134.

154 Frances Hesselbein, in Warren Bennis, *On Becoming a Leader*, Addison-Wesley, Reading, Mass., 1989, page 136.

155 Lao Tzu, in Warren Bennis and Burt Nanus, *Leaders: The Strategies for Taking Charge*, Harper & Row, New York, 1985.

161 Kareem Abdul Jabar with Mignon McCarthy, *Kareem*, Random House, New York, 1990.

Index

A

Action
  commitment and desire required for,
    148–150
  goal setting, 146–148
  integrity gap between beliefs and, 139–
    142
  required of leaders, xvi
  self-assessment prior to, 144–146
  through empowerment/power, 161, 165–
    166
  through strategic thinking, 153–155
Adhocracy: The Power to Change (Waterman),
  2
Akin, Gib, 79, 82
Ambition, 3
Aristotle, *Ethics,* 136
Armstrong, Neil, 165
Assessment, leadership, 14–17

B

Beliefs, gap between action and, 139–142.
  See also Values, personal
Bell, Derek, 144–145
Bennis, Warren
  On Becoming a Leader, 5, 6, 23

description of research by, 22, 99
interview with Frank Dale, 103–104
interview with Ray Kroc, 100
offer to Leon Fleischer, 165
Why Leaders Can't Lead, 45
Berra, Yogi, 2
Blum, Arlene, 111–112
Bureaucracy, 2, 104–105. *See also* Organiza-
  tional environments
Burgher's Daughter, The (Gordimer), xvii
Burke, Jim, 99, 117
Byrom, Fletcher, 83

C

Campbell, Joseph, 4
Casteneda, Carlos, 155
Change
  increasing challenges of, 42–43
  management of, xiii, 2, 134, 153
Change, The (Greer), 23–24
Chorus of Stones, A (Griffin), 63–64
Cleese, John, 83–84
Cleveland, Harlan, *The Knowledge Executive,* 7
Clifford, Clark, 122
Clinton, Bill, 79, 134–135

Index

Cocooning, 43
Comissioná, Sergio, 100–101
Commitment
  exercise for revealing, 150–152
  as fuel for leaders, 32–33
  required for action, 148–150
  to visions, 99–102, 105
Communication
  value of clear, 28
  of visions, xviii, 102–105, 116–118
Companies. *See* Organizational environments
Competencies, 3, 5, 69
Corday, Barbara, 102–103, 150
Coward, Noël, 2
Creativity
  as outcome of failure, 83–84, 95
  process steps, 153–154

D

Dale, Frank, 103–104
Darwin, Charles, 23, 103
Dedication, benefits of, 166
Dempsey, Ellen, xii
DePree, Max
  Leadership Is an Art, 100
  Leadership Jazz, 70–71
  view of leadership role, xv
Desire required for action, 149–150
Diaries (Kafka), 60
Disney, Walt, 102
Diversity of work force, 30
Dockson, Robert, 153
Doctor Zhivago (Pasternak), 132
Drucker, Peter, 100

E

Edelman, Marian Wright, 122
Emerson, Ralph Waldo, 25
Empathy
  description of, 124–125

exercise for practicing, 125–132
leader's use of, 102–103, 120, 125–126
Employees. *See* Work force
Empowerment
  value of, 32, 54, 165–166
  of work force, xviii, 6–7, 165–166
Ethics. *See also* Integrity; Trust
  developing a code of, 135–139
  importance of, 29
Ethics (Aristotle), 136
Everett, Melissa, *Re-Inventing the Corporate Self: The Inner Agenda for Business Transformation,* 139
Exercises, leadership
  analyzing family influences, 60–65
  analyzing leaders in work environments, 64, 66–68
  assessing creativity and failure, 92–95
  assessing qualities for leadership development, 37–40
  common myths about leadership, 51–56
  communicating a personal vision, 116–118
  completing assessment inventory, 14–17
  creating an organizational vision, 105–111
  creating a personal vision, 111–115
  developing a personal agenda, 18–20, 27, 28
  developing group goals, 35–37
  developing leadership through learning, 73–78
  discovering personal patterns of failure, 84–92
  distinguishing between managers and leaders, 9–14
  establishing personal goals, 33–37, 146–148
  evaluating learning modes/styles, 78–82
  evaluating personal code of ethics, 135–139

examining personal history's effects on leadership, 95–98

examining types of power, 161–164

exploring qualities of trust, 121–123

increasing awareness of need for leaders, 56–60

learning from past leaders, 45–51

practicing empathy, 125–132

principled risk takers *versus* conventional decision makers, 139–142

revealing commitments and desires, 150–152

reviewing personal values, 26–33

strategy mapping, 155–161

F

Facilitators, leaders as, 9

Failure

exercise for assessing patterns of, 84–92

handling of, 6, 72, 82–84, 87, 95

Family life's influence on leadership, 60–65

Feedback, 70

Flattening, organizational, xix, xviii, 9, 66. *See also* Organizational environments

Fleischer, Leon, 165

Ford, Henry, xviii, 2

Frady, Marshall, 118

Frankl, Viktor, xi

Friedman, Thomas, 134–135

G

Galileo, 71

Gardner, John, 8–9

No Easy Victories, 135

Gauthier, Alain, 112

Goals. *See also* Objectives, shared; Visions

commitment needed for implementing, 148–149

developing personal leadership agenda, 18–20

exercises for developing, 33–37, 146–148

leader's role in achieving, xv

short-term *versus* long-term, 33

Goldsmith, Joan, 22

Gordimer, Nadine, *The Burgher's Daughter,* xvii

Graham, Katharine, 6

Greer, Germaine, *The Change,* 23–24

Griffin, Susan, *A Chorus of Stones,* 63–64

H

Hare, David, 87

Hesselbein, Frances, 154

Hiatt, Arnold, 95

History of leadership in America, 43–44

Hoffman, Abbie, *Steal This Book,* 24

Horton, R. B., 42

Human Element, The (Schultz), 95

I

Inner voice, 24–25. *See also* Self-reflection

Institutions. *See* Organizational environments

Integrity. *See also* Ethics; Trust

gap between beliefs and actions, 139–142

importance of personal, 2–3, 5, 121

institutional, 42

national, 136

and trust, 132–135

J

Jabar, Kareem Abdul, 161–162

Jackson, Jesse, 118

James, William, 69, 103

Jandernoa, Beth, 112

Jobs, Steven, xviii

K

Kafka, Franz, *Diaries,* 60

Kennedy, John, 79, 116

Kennedy, Robert, 116

Index

King, Martin Luther, Jr., 142
Kirstein, Lincoln, 101–102
Knowledge Executive, The (Cleveland), 7
Kockelmans, Joseph, 133
Krim, Mathilde, 27
Kroc, Ray, 100

L

Laing, R. D., 41
Land, Edwin H., 101
Lao Tzu, 21, 155
Lawrence, T. E., 99
Leaders. *See also* Exercises, leadership
  challenges for, xv–xvi, 1–2
  commitment to vision, 99–102, 105
  creation of, 73–78
  description of, 22, 53, 69, 99, 105, 120–
    121, 144, 153
  ethics of, 135, 136
  importance of, 42
  learning from past models, 45–51
  versus managers, 4–5, 9–14, 14–17, 104
  new role of, xv, 9
  optimism of, xvi
  responses to failure, 82–84
  role of trust, xv–xvi, 3, 5–6, 120, 132–
    135
  strategic thinking of, 153, 155
  turnover and loss of, 41–44
  value of learning, xviii, 165
  values of, 26–33
Leadership. *See also* Exercises, leadership
  action and results required of, xvi
  analyzing role of in work environments,
    64, 66–68
  analyzing the lack of, 56–60
  assessment of personal skills, 14–17
  character-based, xii
  commitment and desire required for ac-
    tion, 148–150

common myths about, 51–56
conditions for success, 3, 4–6, 144
current crisis, xiii–xv, 44–45
development of, 26, 37–40, 45, 70, 73–
  78
empathy and, 102–103, 120, 123–126
family life's influence on, 60–65
historical overview of in America, 43–44
importance of information to, 3
interaction between leaders and followers,
  102
learning of, 7–8, 52, 73–78
organizing "meaning" for others, xv, xviii,
  104–105
paradigm shift, 71–73
purpose of, 2–3
trust and, xv–xvi, 3, 5–6, 120, 132–135
use of empowerment, xviii, 6–7, 32, 54,
  165–166
Leadership Is an Art (DePree), 100
Leadership Jazz (DePree), 70–71
Lear, Norman, 24, 25, 99
Learning
  importance of active, risk-taking experi-
    ences, 73–78
  leadership skills, 7–8, 52, 73–78
  lifelong, 8, 23–24, 70
  modes of, 78–80
  motivations for, 82
  support of in organizational environments,
    xviii–xix
  value of for leaders, xviii, 165
Locke, John, 103
Los Angeles Herald-Examiner, 103–104

M

Machiavelli, Niccolo, 2
Mack, John, *Re-Inventing the Corporate Self:
  The Inner Agenda for Business Transforma-
  tion,* 139

Managers. *See also* Leaders
    versus leaders, 4–5, 9–14, 14–17, 104
    view of change, 2
Man and Superman (Shaw), 101
McKibbon, Lawrence, 25
Meaning created through communication,
    xv, xviii, 103–105
Meyer, Ray, 83
Mission statement. *See* Visions
Mistakes. *See* Failure
Morals. *See* Integrity
Murray, W. H., *The Scottish Himalayan Expe-
    dition*, 148–149

N

No Easy Victories (Gardner), 135

O

Objectives, shared, xviii, 5. *See also* Goals;
    Visions
On Becoming a Leader (Bennis), 5, 6, 23
Optimism, leader's need for, xvi
Oresick, Robert, *Re-Inventing the Corporate
    Self: The Inner Agenda for Business Trans-
    formation*, 139
Organizational environments
    analysis of leadership within, 64, 66–68
    bureaucratic, 2, 104–105
    changing state of, xv, xvii–xix, 9
    dependence upon shared meanings, xv,
      xviii, 104
    elements for success, xvii–xix
    handling of failure, 84
    importance of leadership ethics, 42, 135,
      136
    leadership development in, 25
    nonhierarchical, xix, 9, 66
    role of commitment in, 149
    role of trust in, xv–xvi, 3, 5–6, 120

    use of empowerment, xviii, 6–7, 32,
      165–166
    vision statements for, 106

P

Papp, Joe, 87
Paradigm, shift in leadership, 71–73
Parental Empathy (Paul), 124–125
Passion, 101, 149
Pasternak, Boris, *Doctor Zhivago,* 132
Paul, Norman, *Parental Empathy,* 124–125
Personal values. *See* Values, personal
Peters, Tom, 134
Pollack, Sydney, 5, 124, 153
Porter, Lyman, 25
Power, types of, 161–164

Q

Qualities, leadership. *See also* Empathy; Eth-
    ics; Integrity; Leaders; Leadership; Pas-
    sion; Trust
    exercise for assessing, 37–40
    listing of essential, 144
Quality *versus* quantity, 166

R

Raskin, Jamie, 144, 148
Recognition, on-going, 31
*Re-Inventing the Corporate Self: The Inner
    Agenda for Business Transformation* (Ever-
    ett, Mack and Oresick), 139
Risk-taking behavior, 73–78
Ritchey, Don, 103
Rittenberg, Sidney, 3

S

Schultz, Will, *The Human Element,* 95
Scottish Himalayan Expedition, The (Murray),
    148–149
Sculley, John, 70, 92, 99, 105–106

Index

Self-reflection, 26, 69–71, 144–146
Shakespeare, William, 119
Shaw, George Bernard, 23
    Man and Superman, 101
Steal This Book (Hoffman), 24
Strategic thinking
    benefits of, 153–155
    mapping exercise, 155–161
Strategies for leadership development. *See* Exercises, leadership

T
Taylor, Frederick, 2
Teamwork
    developing group goals, 35–37
    self-managing, 66
    value of, 32, 165
Time, 132–133
Tolstoy, Leo, 101
Training, leadership. *See* Exercises, leadership
Trust. *See also* Ethics; Integrity
    characteristics of, xv–xvi, 120, 133–134
    exercise for assessing, 121–123
    role of, xv–xvi, 3, 5–6, 120
    through integrity, 132–135
Tunney, John, 116

V
Vail, Theodore, xviii
Values, personal. *See also* Ethics; Integrity
    clear communication, 28
    diverse work force, 30
    empowerment, 32
    ethical practices, 29
    exercise for reflection on, 26–28
    on-going recognition, 31
Vision(s). *See also* Goals
    alignment and communication of, xviii, 102–105, 116–118

conditions for successful implementation of, 3, 4–5
creating an organizational, 105–111
creating a personal, 111–115
definition of, 105, 106
leader's commitment to, 99–102, 105
supported by empathy, 124
supported by trust, 120

W
Wallenda, Karl, 82–83
Waterman, Bob, *Adhocracy: The Power to Change,* 2
Weber, Max, 2
West, Cornel, 1
When Work Disappears (Wilson), xiii
White, E. B., xii
Why Leaders Can't Lead (Bennis), 45
Wilde, Oscar, 148
Williams, Harold, 134
Wilson, Blenda, 143–144
Wilson, Larry, 149
Wilson, William Julius, *When Work Disappears,* xiii
Women
    empathy and, 102–103
    empowerment of, xviii
    leadership through lifelong learning, 23–24
    power of visions, 111–112
Wooden, John, 161–162
Work force. *See also* Employees
    analysis of leadership within, 64, 66–68
    diversity of, 30
    effects of vision on, 101
    empowerment of, xviii, 6–7, 165–166
Workplace. *See* Organizational environment
Wozniak, Steve, xviii